How to Love
Your Retirement

WARNING:

This guide contains differing opinions. Hundreds of Heads will not always agree. Advice taken in combination may cause unwanted side effects. Use your head when selecting advice.

How to Love Your Retirement
The Guide to the Best of Your Life

Barbara Waxman, MS, MPA
Special Editor

Hundreds of Heads Books, LLC
ATLANTA, GEORGIA

Cover images © istockphoto.com
Book design by Elizabeth Johnsboen

Pages 100-102 excerpted from the book *Younger Next Year: A Guide to Living Like 50 Until You're 80 and Beyond* by Christopher Crowley and Henry S. Lodge, © 2004, 2005. Reprinted with permission of the author.

Pages 60-62 © 2010 Julie Lopp. All rights reserved.
Pages 253-268 © The Odyssey Group. Used with permission.

Library of Congress Cataloging-in-Publication Data
How to love your retirement : the guide to the "best" of your life / Barbara Waxman, special editor. -- 2nd ed.

      p. cm.
 ISBN 978-1-933512-89-1
 1. Retirement--United States. 2. Retirees--United States--Life skills guides. I. Waxman, Barbara Frey.
 HQ1063.2.U6H68 2010
 646.7'90973--dc22

                                                           2010025115

See pages 273-274 for credits.

HUNDREDS OF HEADS® books are available at special discounts when purchased in bulk for premiums or institutional or educational use. Excerpts and custom editions can be created for specific uses. For more information, please email sales@hundredsofheads.com or write to:

HUNDREDS OF HEADS BOOKS, LLC
#230
2221 Peachtree Road, Suite D
Atlanta, Georgia 30309

ISBN: 978-19335128-9-1

Printed in Canada
10 9 8 7 6 5 4 3 2 1

Mixed Sources
Product group from well-managed forests and other controlled sources
www.fsc.org Cert no. SW-COC-000952
© 1996 Forest Stewardship Council
FSC

CONTENTS

INTRODUCTION

What is retirement in the 21st century?

We hear about the longevity revolution all the time: In 1900, the average life expectancy at birth was 47 years; babies born today can expect to live to age 78. Today a man at age 65 can expect to live another 17 years; a woman can expect another 20 years. And if you exercise, remain active and engaged, and don't smoke, living to 100 might be a reality. While these tremendous gains are something we have wanted they come with some challenges. If you think about it, what we have really gained is not more years at the end of our lives, but additional active years in midlife. And knowing how to navigate these new and robust years can be daunting. Fear not: the hundreds of people interviewed in this book share some vital advice for this stage, when work is no longer the primary activity, and a sense of adventure, meaning and purpose takes on an even greater role.

As originally envisioned during the Depression, retirement moved people out of the workforce to make room for younger workers. The question was, what to do with those 10 or so years? Dell Webb and others answered the question with the development of retirement communities based around leisure and made up of people all around the same age. As a result, retirement quickly became synonymous with three primary ideas: playing golf (or something of that sort); taking that vacation you've always dreamed of; and spending time with grandchildren. That was about it.

That model doesn't work anymore. Simply put, we need to retire the word retirement! The new retirement, or *pro-tirement*, means ending the traditional way we have worked at our full-time jobs and venturing into new ways of using our time. If you think of your life as a portfolio of activities, much like your financial portfolio, consider how you invest your time. Up until now you may have invested the majority of your portfolio into work. With careful retirement planning—*not* the financial kind—you can reallocate your time spent on activities/relationships that you choose in a way that designs your personal portfolio of meaningful choices. Many people assume that retirement means not doing any work in exchange for compensation. Not so: retirement may mean starting a new home-based business or working part-time; it does not necessarily mean a cessation of work for pay. In fact, given our extended life expectancy, many people need to maintain an income stream in retirement. The difference is really based on the centrality of work in your life.

Retirement is also about purpose, passion and the place where the two intersect. It's about strengthening bonds with friends, family members and those causes that we relate to. It's about a peak quality of life.

Retirement may look like an inspired phase of creativity where you finally take up an instrument, sing in a choir, develop your inner artist, write your memoir—who knows? We do know this: creativity, lifelong learning and engaging in activities and with people who make you smile will increase not only the quantity but also the quality of your years.

Retirement may get you into the best physical shape of your life. Retirees are competing in Senior Olympics, climbing mountains, and generally feeling more engaged and energized than when they were younger. Some are experiencing their most creative and productive years ever.

Retirement also signifies change, and if there is one thing we've learned it's that change is never easy. We'll introduce you to an effective model for change that will help demystify some of your feelings and move you toward the balance you desire in your life.

Don't expect to know exactly what this stage will look like for you. Experiment. Discover new things by taking a risk and signing up for that class you've always wondered about. Offer your help in an area you'd like to learn more about by creating an adult internship. Remember, 60 really is the new 45! In these pages, hundreds of individuals tell us just how they are transforming their retirement phase in new and exciting ways. Experts in critical subject areas offer tips, information and perspective on this Third Stage. Welcome to what *will* be some of the best years of your life.

BARBARA WAXMAN
Founder, The Odyssey Group

21st-Century Retirement: The Third Stage

One of the most exciting aspects of 21st-century retirement is that today's baby boomers, those born between 1946 and 1964, are in the midst of giving yesterday's retirement a complete overhaul. That isn't surprising when you consider the fact that boomers have influenced our society since birth. The proliferation of suburbia was fed by America's growing families. In addition to changing society's structure, the boomers' effect on civil rights, women's rights, sexual rights and so much more, has created an entirely new way to experience life. In short, boomers have always claimed the freedom to choose their own path. Retirement is no different.

Today's retirees are blazing new trails. Look at colleges bursting with older adults. Look at gyms filled with mid-lifers. Look at organizations (both volunteer and for pay) that are actively recruiting for part-time support. Retirement—or better yet, "pro-tirement"—is a time of renewal, growth, meaning and purpose.

How do you know when it's time to retire? First, and perhaps most obviously, you must understand your financial needs. Although this is not a financial planning book—there are plenty of good ones out there—see Chapter 7 for more on this topic. Assuming you are able to transition from your current income to a lesser one or none at all, ask yourself this question: Has work become less of a contribution and a meaningful way to spend your time, or what one client of mine unhappily referred to as "having to go to the J-O-B"? Of course, no one loves work all of the time, but if there exists a sense of calling to something else or to a constellation of other activities, I suggest you dip a toe in the water and try it out. Retirement need not be an ending, with a gold-watch ceremony, but can be a negotiated withdrawal from a position over time. Experiment with it and own your future.

I HAD BEEN THINKING ABOUT RETIREMENT FOR SOME TIME, but really couldn't make up my mind to quit a job I truly loved. My relationships with my students meant so much to me that I was afraid I'd miss them terribly if I retired. I thought about it and prayed about it. Finally, God got tired of listening to me and gave me a shove. I lost my voice; for a teacher, that can be disastrous. I thought I had laryngitis, but found out it was something else and that it wasn't going to clear up on its own. Now, after three years of regular treatment, I have my voice back most of the time. God knew what I needed, even if I didn't.

—SUSAN
TAYLOR, TEXAS
YEARS RETIRED: 3

- - - - - - - -

RETIREMENT SOUNDS SO TERMINAL, but it's really just the end of one part of life and the beginning of another. It's a transition from part one to part two. Some people do it gradually. When I knew I was going to retire a year ago, I already felt like I was retired, so I was trying out things like playing with investments and hobbies.

—GARY SMITH
SAN ANTONIO, TEXAS
YEARS RETIRED: 1

- - - - - - - -

WORKING AND BEING INVOLVED AND PASSIONATE about something is a very important part of living. Otherwise you are just an eating machine. You can get up in the morning and have coffee, go on the computer, meet a friend for lunch or belong to organizations, but that doesn't seem very exciting to me. I don't care if I live two years, one year or 10 years more.

—SUE SIEGAL
SAN FRANCISCO, CALIFORNIA

- - - - - - - -

THE RIGHT TIME TO RETIRE is when you have more things to do outside of work than you have time to do while working.

—YITZ
MANCHESTER, UNITED KINGDOM
YEARS RETIRED: 8

I HAD BEEN PREPARING FOR RETIREMENT. My accounting and management-consulting firm that I worked for had a requirement that any partner had to retire by age 60. I wanted to continue in the management consulting business, but not on a full-time basis. So I made some calls to former associates, and I formed what I called the Strategy Facilitation Group. This helped me prepare for retirement. I was very organized; it's my nature. The result was, I had some work lined up before I left the firm. The difference was, I was able to call my own shots. It was part-time and I was no longer bound to the things you are often required to do when working for a company.

—*Barry Mundt*
Asheville, North Carolina
Years retired: 14

• • • • • • • •

BY THE AGE OF 65, most of us have accomplished whatever work-related goals we are going to reach. If you haven't done it by then, chances are you aren't going to do it. Take the retirement, take the pension, take the Social Security, and sail off into the sunset.

—*Sue Lasky*
Poland, Ohio

• • • • • • • •

I DID NOT GET MUCH CHOICE ON MY RETIREMENT. They came to me when I was 59 1/2 and told me that if I didn't retire, they were going to take away about $40,000 a year in pay. I had planned to stay until I was 62, but I couldn't afford not to go.

—*Lawrence "Bimp" Layman*
Harrisonburg, Virginia
Years retired: 1

• • • • • • • •

I WANTED TO TOTALLY CHANGE MY LIFE AROUND. They say you have a new life waiting, and I wanted to be young enough to enjoy it.

—*J.L.*
Jackson, New Jersey
Years retired: 2

I WAS A PEDIATRIC NURSE-PRACTITIONER FOR 25 YEARS, and before I turned 60, I thought I would work until I was 90. I loved my job so much! After I turned 60, I found I was just getting so tired. Sixty really seems to be a turning point for people, a time when they really start thinking about retirement. So I decided to retire and was able to phase myself out over a six-month period.

—*CYNTHIA*
ST. PAUL, MINNESOTA
YEARS RETIRED: 8

PLAN AHEAD

If retirement is on your horizon, come up with a list of post-retirement activities in advance and, if necessary, take time *before* you retire to acquire skills you can use in your post-retirement life.

THE BABY-BOOM GENERATION has redefined every decade of their lives. And we are living differently than any humans have ever lived on the planet, and our children are an offshoot of that. We blazed the trails; we never accepted the status quo. And we're moving forward and now we're redefining retirement.

—*CINDY JOSEPH*
NEW YORK, NEW YORK

A GOOD FRIEND OF MINE ONCE SAID, "You'll know when the time comes." For me, I was having health problems. But also, my whole office had been computerized, and it was a struggle for me. I couldn't even type! It was my time.

—*JOHN R. BRIGHT*
ALLENTOWN, PENNSYLVANIA
YEARS RETIRED: 10

TWO YEARS BEFORE I WANTED TO RETIRE, my company informed me that it no longer needed my job. As part of my severance package, I received one month's salary for every year of employment. Altogether, this amounted to 18 months of pay. In contrast, if I'd continued working for those two years and retired on my own terms, I would've received nothing. Sometimes, it really is better to retire according to your company's schedule!

—*ANONYMOUS*
CORVALLIS, OREGON
YEARS RETIRED: 11

MAKE THE MOST OUT OF YOUR WORKING YEARS

According to a study by the Employee Benefit Research Institute, Minnesota has the highest level of participation in employment-based retirement plans. Florida, Georgia and California came in last.

MY BROTHER WENT INTO THE HOSPITAL FOR ROUTINE SURGERY. He got an infection and died a few weeks later. His sudden death made my husband and me realize that we were getting older. We wanted to spend time together and have fun while we were healthy. He was the one who suggested that we retire, but I agreed. It was the best decision we could have made. We love not having to get up and go to work.

—*DONNA HANAFIN*
NIXA, MISSOURI

WHEN THEY TALK ABOUT YOUR GOLDEN YEARS, this is what they're talking about.

—*MARIO ONCEY*
POLAND, OHIO

I FIGURED IF I WAITED NINE MORE YEARS UNTIL I TURNED 65, I wouldn't be able to do some of the things I could do at 56. These extra years have given my husband and me valuable extra time to see the country and do things we were never able to do before.

> —*G.M.*
> *CUMBERLAND, MARYLAND*
> *YEARS RETIRED: 4*

I WAS DIAGNOSED WITH LEUKEMIA, a fairly aggressive form. I had every intention of living into my 90s, like my dad and his dad, and I'm not going to make that now. But it caused us to rethink how we prepare for the years ahead. We had a 30-year game plan. We now realize we need to have a five-year game plan. What things are really important to us— friends we want to stay in touch with, places we want to travel? It's easy to say we'll do that someday, but you never know when the opportunity is going to be taken away. And rather than be morbid or negative, it's important that people be realistic and try to set some short-term, medium-term, and long-term goals.

> —*FRED TEACH*
> *CANDLER, NORTH CAROLINA*
> *YEARS RETIRED: 3*

I KNEW I WANTED TO HAVE A CERTAIN LIFESTYLE when I retired, and I sat down with a financial planner who gave us a very good list to think about what we spend money on. It really helped. You just have to focus, think about what you are going to do, what kind of finances you need, and do it.

> —*E.M.*
> *EDGEWATER, NEW JERSEY*
> *YEARS RETIRED: 3*

I DON'T THINK THERE IS A SINGLE BEST AGE for someone to retire. I think that it's as individual as we are.

> —*SUSAN*
> *TAYLOR, TEXAS*
> *YEARS RETIRED: 3*

The Coach's Corner

7 STEPS TO THE PERFECT "PRO-TIREMENT"

Retirement planning used to be all about getting your finances in order, but that exclusivity has left many people feeling at a loss. Counselors have found that those people who focused on finances without also focusing on life in general have started their retirement strong, but then found that their retirement felt less purposeful and less enjoyable than expected. The good news is that there is a new way to think about retirement planning, in addition to crunching numbers. Here are my steps to a perfect protirement:

1. **Less is more.** Simplify your possessions, your activities and your relationships. Here's a good rule of thumb: If it energizes you, keep it; if it leaves you feeling depleted, release it.

2. **Live within your means.** By this time you have crunched the numbers and determined what your post-traditional career income will be. Create a budget including travel, leisure, eating out, and education, and certainly accounting for future health care costs so that you can be fiscally responsible by day and sleep better at night.

3. **Stay fit.** If you have not established an exercise routine, now is the perfect time. Exercise in a way that leaves you feeling great, both emotionally and physically. Whether you want to train for a marathon or just learn to stretch, make physical activity part of your daily routine.

4. **Bolster your brain health.** Research has shown that our brains remain capable of making new connections throughout life. Engage in meaningful activities, or learn a new language or skill; you'll find yourself less apt to complain about 'senior moments.'

5. **Live your values.** Clarify and list them, from ethical qualities, like integrity, truth and compassion, to those aspects you want in your life on a regular basis, like friendship, humor and service. Use those values as a kind of litmus test for your life. Are you living your values? Are you surrounding yourself with others who share them? Living your values is like an insurance policy against depression.

6. **Laugh.** You know this from experience: Humor has the power to reduce stress and enhance one's sense of well-being. Research has shown that laughter improves pain tolerance, reduces anxiety, promotes a sense of well-being, and even increases the oxygen level in the blood, which helps memory and physical health.

7. **Give.** When we offer our time and ourselves we reap far more than we give. As Albert Schweitzer once said, "I don't know what your destiny will be, but one thing I do know; the only ones among you who will be really happy are those who have sought and found how to serve."

—B.W.

I RETIRED WHEN I WAS 60, which is really quite a luxury. I was able to access some of my retirement funds, and my husband, who had been working part-time, was really ready to retire. Also, I wanted to have time to spend with my mother; we ended up having three years when we could go shopping every week, and I'm so glad I was able to do that. And finally, I felt like I was going out at the top of my game, not when I was sick of the job and all my coworkers.

—Jeanne
Minneapolis, Minnesota
Years retired: 7

I WORKED AT *THE NEW YORK TIMES* and was head of the news research staff that provides information to reporters and editors for breaking news and long-term projects. I loved the job and the intensity of the newsroom. It was an electric charge just walking into the place, and of course my colleagues were interesting and friendly. I also did some books for *The Times* in my spare time, and wrote a couple of columns, including the weekly news quiz, which ran in the Saturday edition for over a decade. I was ready to retire, in part because I was over 65, but also because the technology kept getting increasingly complex. I started with, basically, books and a telephone when I went into the field. I then used databases, of course, but wound up saying, "I see the pixels on the wall," and decided that it was time to leave. Before I left, I made a deal to do two more cookbooks for them. So I was immediately working on a book. It gave me work I enjoyed and it gave me focus. That transitioned me from full-time work to not working.

—*LINDA AMSTER*
NEW YORK, NEW YORK
YEARS RETIRED: 5

• • • • • • • •

I AM RETIRED, IN THE SENSE THAT I am no longer in that business full time, running a company. But I am not retiring from life. As I was about to sell my company in 1999, I realized I had a lot of time that I was hopefully going to be alive after that. So I constructed a little format in outline form called "ideas for semi-retirement," and I sat down at my computer and said, "Who am I?" There was my personal life, my business life and philanthropy. Then I figured out what in each of those different categories I had an interest in at that moment; the idea was that it was a living document, a temporary thing, and from time to time I would change the content within the categories.

—*BOB WALDORF*
LOS ANGELES, CALIFORNIA
YEARS RETIRED: 11

RETIRE SOONER RATHER THAN LATER. Do not let financial issues dictate when you retire. Let your excitement for the job dictate when you leave it. If you are burned out, hating the job, or too stressed, leave it and get another job if you have to. Work part-time if you can't afford to completely retire. The stress of a job that you're not enjoying will have physical effects on the body.

—*FRANK HAWK*
LAKELAND, FLORIDA
YEARS RETIRED: 3

• • • • • • • •

I DID NOT PLAN FOR RETIREMENT IN ANY ORGANIZED WAY. I just thought that retirement would give me time to travel and time to take the Master Gardener training course, which I had long wanted to do.

—*ANONYMOUS*
NEVADA
YEARS RETIRED: 13

• • • • • • • •

MY HUSBAND TOOK AN EARLY RETIREMENT at the age of 56. His health continued to gradually go downhill, and as I continued to work long hours at a large university, I saw that these were going to be his best years and that I better grab them before we would have no fun time for each other. I truly loved my job and always thought they would have to kick me out the door. The plan was to work part-time for one year and then retire. But as I was training my replacement, we received a call from our daughter in Boston: her husband had been diagnosed with a brain tumor. Our world was turned upside down! I walked out of the office that day and never looked back. Luckily our son-in-law had a great outcome and continues to do well today. But that was the real hit of how unexpectedly short life can be, and that we had better enjoy every minute!

—*BEVERLY*
ATLANTA, GEORGIA
YEARS RETIRED: 4

MY CAREER IN EDUCATION ESTABLISHED a fixed pension based on 34 years of service, which gave me full benefits. Things like health insurance, Roth IRAs, tax-sheltered annuities, and daughters getting married are not fixed items, but they all are certainly a part of the decision. I retired at age 58, but knew I was ready to retire several years before. Planning was essential, and that is probably the number one skill I learned in my profession—plan ahead!

—DEE
OAK LAWN, ILLINOIS
YEARS RETIRED: 1

• • • • • • • •

MY SITUATION IS A LITTLE DIFFERENT THAN MOST: I am retired from the military. I put in my 20 years and then got the heck out. When I tell people I'm retired, they look at me funny because I'm only 46.

—TAMMY NELSON
MIDLOTHIAN, MARYLAND
YEARS RETIRED: 3

• • • • • • • •

I PROBABLY NEVER WOULD HAVE RETIRED if I hadn't started dating a new boyfriend, who had a house up in New Hampshire. I felt like I was getting older, and I was having such a good time with him. I wanted to enjoy going up there together, which was tough with the amount of vacation you get in life. I'm sure if I had said something to my boss, I could have worked a couple of days a week, but I loved going up for the whole summer, and I don't think that would have been possible.

—SONYA
BROOKLYN, NEW YORK
YEARS RETIRED: 10

• • • • • • • • •

THIRTY WAS MY MAGIC NUMBER. Once I hit 30 years of service, I was outta there.

—KAREN WEAVER
LANCASTER, PENNSYLVANIA
YEARS RETIRED: 2

THE NUMBER ONE THING IS TO MAKE UP YOUR MIND that you're retiring when you do. Know that it is a very significant step and make it permanent—don't dabble in going back. If you keep trying to touch back into what you did, even if you are volunteering, you'll find fault in how your job is now being done.

—*MARGARET MCCOWN*
JACKSONVILLE, TEXAS
YEARS RETIRED: 16

• • • • • • • •

I WOULD HAVE LIKED TO RETIRE GRADUALLY, but as a nurse in a hospital, all the technological changes and procedures became overwhelming. I was very relieved when I quit. If you can retire gradually, it will be much more enjoyable. As you age, you lose energy and get tired, and you realize that you can't do everything.

—*J.L.*
MINNEAPOLIS, MINNESOTA
YEARS RETIRED: 10

• • • • • • • •

TAKE CONTROL

People who retire by choice enjoy happier retirements than those who are forced to stop working, whether due to illness or layoffs. The difference in satisfaction levels can be seen for up to 10 years.

• • • • • • • •

IT IS UNWISE TO THINK YOU CAN PLAN YOUR RETIREMENT with any exactitude. Unexpected events crop up, and sometimes you have to change course a bit. But don't sweat it; go with the flow.

—*B.L.*
SAN JOSE, CALIFORNIA
YEARS RETIRED: 8

ON MY FIRST DAY OF RETIREMENT, I slept late, ate brunch out, and then just sloughed around the house all day with my guys (dog and husband). This was after joyriding during the hot summer day at noontime with the sunroof open, the windows down, and the radio blaring, just because we could.

—*C.R.*
SAN ANTONIO, TEXAS
YEARS RETIRED: 1

• • • • • • • •

I WAS OFFERED AN INCENTIVE PLAN TO RETIRE that included a half year of pay. I was 63 years old. I started working when I was nine years old, sweeping at the local grocery store before school. I worked hard all of my life; I decided it was time to enjoy it. You should take advantage of the opportunity to do the things you love while you are in good health.

—*JOHN BECKER*
SPRINGFIELD, MISSOURI
YEARS RETIRED: 12

• • • • • • • •

I RETIRED COLD TURKEY. I was tired of the structured work environment after 40 years and wanted a clean break. I am tempted to say that maybe I should have worked for another three years, until 65, but this would have been just to save more money and draw a higher Social Security check. And I would have found those additional three years a real grind.

—*B.L.*
SAN JOSE, CALIFORNIA
YEARS RETIRED: 8

• • • • • • • •

WE CAME FROM A GENERATION that saw no stops and we still see no stops. My generation, the baby boomer generation, came of age in the 1960s. We felt very empowered. Everything we wanted to change seemed to change. We thought, 'we can do it'. We just never thought differently.

—*JOAN*
SAN FRANCISCO, CALIFORNIA
YEARS RETIRED: LESS THAN 1

WHEN YOU FINALLY GET SICK OF ALL THE BS, it's time to retire. As an assistant principal, I wanted to make certain changes. Specifically, I wanted to involve the community with our school by developing more family-oriented activities. Unfortunately, there were all these roadblocks (read: other people) who wouldn't allow it. I simply didn't have the energy to fight anymore. I'd been working for 32 years, and I knew retirement was just around the corner anyway, so I figured, why not do it now?

—JEFFREY WACO
NEW YORK, NEW YORK
YEARS RETIRED: 2

LOCATION, LOCATION

Where you live may influence how you feel about and prepare for retirement. Pre-retirees in the West are the most positive about retirement. For example, they have the highest level of optimism (87%) compared to other regions, and nine out of ten expect to be happy in their future retirement.

More pre-retired Westerners (66%) have determined the amount of income they need for their retirement than their counterparts in the Northeast (43%), Midwest (51%) and the South (50%). Pre-retirees in the West were better read and informed about retirement (66%) than those in the South and Northeast (trailing at 52%).

Westerners (76%), Northeasterners (75%) and Midwesterners (75%) beat out Southern pre-retirees (61%) in setting aside more money in their savings and investments.

I WORKED IN CONSTRUCTION MY WHOLE LIFE, and the work just got to be too much for me physically. That's really a younger man's work, but it was the only thing I ever did and the only thing I knew how to do. After I turned 50, I really started to feel the aches and pains more frequently. At the end of each week, I'd really be hurting. Luckily, I had saved enough money and my wife has a good enough job that I could call it quits.

—*RAY VINCET*
LAVALE, MARYLAND
YEARS RETIRED: 3

* * * * * * * *

TIMING IS EVERYTHING

Deciding when to retire is no longer pegged to a particular age, such as when Social Security benefits become available. Today, retirement appears to be a much more personal decision. The most often cited retirement trigger was a feeling of financial independence or freedom. Also among the most significant triggers for retirement were a significant birthday and a serious health issue or illness.

* * * * * * * *

WE STARTED PLANNING FOR RETIREMENT TWO YEARS before we did it. We explored, looking for a place we would want to settle. Weather was a factor: We had a great vacation home in Maine where we liked to spend the summer, but in the winter, there was usually about 20 feet of snow, and that wasn't something that seemed appealing. We found some land in Seattle and started the building process. We retired, moved in, and did the finishing work ourselves.

—*GEORGE RIES*
SEATTLE, WASHINGTON
YEARS RETIRED: 30

I HAD BEEN TEACHING 36 YEARS, and I was just going through the motions. I met with a financial consultant about retirement planning and found out that I'd be taking home more money after retiring. My paycheck now is larger; it was a great opportunity!

> —*DANIEL DIMATTEO*
> *MILLER PLACE, NEW YORK*
> *YEARS RETIRED: 4*

I WAS GOING TO CONTINUE WORKING A LITTLE LONGER, but then things changed suddenly: The universe wanted me out sooner. I was having problems with my heart. I didn't really feel like there was much of a choice. I could have stayed a little longer, but I decided that, rather than waiting and leaving because of health issues a few months down the road, I should at least embrace where I was being sent next. Either way, the universe was going to get me where I am now: retirement. It's important for people to acknowledge when there are forces greater than their conscious minds affecting their decisions, and to realize there's no way to fight them.

> —*MICHAEL*
> *SAYVILLE, NEW YORK*
> *YEARS RETIRED: 1*

RETIRE AS SOON AS YOU CAN DO IT FINANCIALLY. Don't be a hero. Enjoy the time you have left.

> —*DOM GRECO*
> *POLAND, OHIO*

MY DECISION TO RETIRE WAS PARTLY HEALTH-RELATED. After going through breast cancer surgery, I no longer know what my life expectancy is. I want to enjoy whatever time I have left now while I still can.

> —*KATHY*
> *WASHINGTON, D.C.*
> *YEARS RETIRED: 1*

PARTY TIME

Every rite of passage deserves celebration. Including retirement. You deserve to be rewarded for all those years of hard work (and to celebrate the fact that you'll no longer be doing it).

I TOLD TWO PERSONAL STORIES WHEN I spoke at my retirement party. One was very funny, and the other one was extremely meaningful to the people who worked at the hospital I was retiring from. Try to tell a personal story that is really meaningful that happened to you at the institution. It will resonate with people you are saying goodbye to. We're all trying to find meaning in life. It's good to tell a funny story, too.

> —ROY CLARY
> BROOKLYN, NEW YORK
> YEARS RETIRED: 1

WHEN THE SUBJECT OF MY RETIREMENT PARTY CAME UP, I told people in my department that if I had to choose, I would choose not to have one. People in the department said, "We don't care whether you come or not. We're having one." Just take it all in and enjoy it. My retirement party had about 100 people. The secretaries in the department were the primary organizers. They wrote to several colleagues and asked for letters, which were included in the book that was given to me. They had pictures of me over time that showed that we do, indeed, get older. They invited all of my children and stepchildren. They all said nice things. My wife was there to greet people with me. The department gave me some small gifts and humorous gifts. There were snacks and a cake and punch. It was a very nice affair.

> —ROBERT L. ZIMDAHL
> FORT COLLINS, COLORADO
> YEARS RETIRED: 1

MAKE SURE THAT PEOPLE ARE WELL AWARE of your post-retirement plans when you have a retirement party. At my retirement party, we had big signs that listed all the places I wanted to go in retirement. It gave us all something to talk about. It felt like people weren't saying goodbye but were saying, "Bon voyage ... we'll see you when you get back!"

—AARON
ST. PETERSBURG, FLORIDA
YEARS RETIRED: 2

I WAS TEMPORARILY RETIRED WHEN I suffered an injury and had to give up my dental practice. At this time, the enforced schedule resulted in a complete relaxation of my previously uptight personality. For the first time in my life, I was not under pressure to produce an income that would support the household. Because it was out of my hands, and I had no choice, I was able to use the time to unwind and focus on the things I really enjoyed. In a way, it was a blessing.

—ANONYMOUS
TORONTO, ONTARIO
YEARS RETIRED: 10

. . . .

WHEN I WAS ABOUT 58 I began working as a grant writer. Of course, I'd written grant proposals before but not as my main job description. It was nice to get a paycheck after free-lancing for so long, but I didn't think of it as a career, with the kind of ambitions you have when you are younger. It's nice to go to an office with nice people and free coffee. I think the people I work with sort of like it that I'm an old guy; I remind them of their fathers. I'm not crazy, like other people obsessed with their own agendas sometimes are. My agenda is the paycheck and working this job for a few more years and exiting gracefully. This is my last job; I'm not looking toward moving up.

—PETER
MINNEAPOLIS, MINNESOTA

HOW DID I KNOW WHEN IT WAS TIME TO RETIRE? My wife told me! I was teaching at a university in San Angelo, Texas. My wife took a teaching job in El Paso. For about two years we commuted back and forth on the weekends; it was about a six-and-a-half-hour drive. I knew it was time to retire when my wife said, "I've been following you around for 30 years! Now it's time for you to follow me!" So I retired from my university job and moved to El Paso.

> —ANONYMOUS
> EL PASO, TEXAS
> YEARS RETIRED: 2

* * * * * * * *

AFTER YOU RETIRE, ALLOW YOURSELF TO VEG OUT for at least three months after leaving the busy working world. Just hang out. Don't make any specific plans; be spontaneous and do what you feel like doing. Give the things in your heart time to bubble up and help you decide what your priorities will be in your retirement years. Decide what means the most to you and what you really feel passionate about. Then go for it big-time.

> —EMILY KIMBALL
> RICHMOND, VIRGINIA

* * * * * * * *

I NEVER THOUGHT I WOULD RETIRE: I had no models for retirement. In my family, for two generations, nobody retired. Nobody said they were retired: nobody moved to a retirement community; nobody had hobbies to retire to.

> —PAULA
> VANCOUVER, B.C., CANADA
> YEARS RETIRED: 3

* * * * * * * *

PEOPLE ARE REWRITING THE CODE ON what retirement and older living styles look like: It's an un-retiring. We baby boomers and children of the '60s wanted to live as fully as we could. I've been in an evolutionary journey of how I have been living my life. I have been able to learn what's calling me and be brave enough to step into that calling.

> —MARCIA JAFFE
> MILL VALLEY, CALIFORNIA

WE'RE NOT SITTING IN ROCKING CHAIRS on the front porch. We're running marathons and becoming yoga teachers and traveling the world. We're just as alive and active now as we were in our 20s.

—*CINDY JOSEPH*
NEW YORK, NEW YORK

. . . .

WHEN YOU HAVE ENOUGH MONEY to live for the rest of your life without working, that's when you know it's time to retire. For some people, that might be when they're 30. Others might not hit this point until they're 93. For me, it happened in my 60s.

—*GARY GALLAGHER*
WILLIAMSON, WEST VIRGINIA
YEARS RETIRED: 1

. . . .

I'VE USED WORDS LIKE REPOTTING. Every once in a while you need to repot. Either your roots are outgrowing the pot, or you get a bigger pot. Things get tired and you just need to freshen up the soil.

—*MITCH COHEN*
MILL VALLEY, CALIFORNIA
YEARS RETIRED: 2

The "R" Word: Feelings and Attitudes

Most of us have followed the path we thought would lead to success. We worked hard in school, got a good first job and worked our way up, got married and had a family, worked some more. Now we should know what we want next: some travel, some golf, some time with grandchildren and that's it. Right?

Not necessarily. Some of us want to spend this large chunk of our lives without many commitments aside from leisure, and there are millions more who yearn for something more goal-oriented and more meaningful, in the legacy sense of the word. What has become so clear to me in my coaching work is that the feelings and attitudes we have about retirement are in the midst of changing. Today's generation of people eligible for retirement are healthier, tend to be wealthier and are better educated than ever before. They want more than what they have traditionally seen as retirement but have few role models to follow. That leaves many people confused. They wonder: How do I define myself during this retirement stage? What do I want to do with my time? What if I just want to relax for a while—must I do something important? What if I want to find a whole new *occupation—is it too late? After pondering questions like these, one of our interviewees described his impending retirement as feeling as though he would be "falling off of a cliff".*

It was not so long ago that "retirement"—the days between the conclusion of our formal working years or years spent raising a family, and either death or decrepitude—lasted perhaps a decade: not long enough to really concern oneself with much more than leisure and some family time. Now the years we've added to our lives don't show up so much at the end as they do in the middle. Much of my retirement coaching work has been to help people identify what they want to do when they grow up— whether they are 50, 60 or 70 years old. And through this work I have come to agree wholeheartedly with something stated in the inspiring book, Success Built to Last: Creating a Life that Matters: "Success in the long run has less to do with finding the best idea, organizational structure, or business model for an enterprise, than with discovering what matters to us as individuals." When we are clear about what matters, we find, as another interviewee pointed out, that our CV may in fact shorten with age—we spend our time more wisely, doing work that matters.

I NEVER HEARD OF THE WORD, RETIREMENT. I know my father never heard of that word, and that's probably why I'm not familiar with it. What exactly does that mean? I picture a bunch of old geezers sitting around playing gin rummy in rocking chairs with afghans over their laps: No, thank you. That's not for me. I plan to get up every day and get my hands dirty until God calls me home.

> —*MITZIE HAGEN*
> *WHEELING, WEST VIRGINIA*
> *YEARS RETIRED: 4*

TO ENJOY YOUR RETIREMENT, you have to be able to feel useful, needed, wanted and valuable.

> —*BARRY BIANCO*
> *BRISTOL, WISCONSIN*
> *YEARS RETIRED: 2*

IDLE HANDS

Retirees who go back to work part-time or decide to volunteer reportedly feel happier than those who stay at home.

IF YOU'RE GOING TO RETIRE, you need activities to keep you sharp. My plan was to open a kayak-touring business based out of a family vacation home in New Hampshire. It has been a little more difficult than I expected, but I'm doing it. And I've found it's nice to have something to do for six months a year.

> —*FRED*
> *MILLER PLACE, NEW YORK*
> *YEARS RETIRED: 2*

I DON'T BELIEVE IN RETIREMENT. Retooling yourself is the idea.

> —*MICHAEL CREEDMAN*
> *SAN FRANCISCO, CALIFORNIA*

PEOPLE WHO ARE NOT RETIRED THINK there is just nothing for the retired person to do at this point in their life. Well, forget that, folks! I have time to help many family members or neighbors who need that little extra aid for whatever reason. For me, it means caregiving for my aging parents; then there is taking care of the house, the car, pets, and sometimes, late at night, enjoying those moments called "leisure" for retirees!

> —*L.H.*
> *SAN ANTONIO, TEXAS*
> *YEARS RETIRED: 1*

KEEPING BUSY

An AARP study showed that approximately 70% of baby boomers intend to work full- or part-time while they collect their pensions.

SITTING HOME, READING THE PAPER, and watching TV is great for about one week!

> —*ROY CLARY*
> *BROOKLYN, NEW YORK*
> *YEARS RETIRED: 1*

I MADE TIME A HIGH PRIORITY—more than owning a home, more than career—because time is the one thing you don't get more of. Bill Gates can't buy more time. For me the whole idea of retirement is really to have the freedom to do what you really want to do, which means knowing your values, knowing what will really make you feel happy, and knowing and feeling that your life has a purpose.

> —*MARC GOLD*
> *BANGKOK, THAILAND*

I FIND THAT SO MANY PEOPLE, MYSELF INCLUDED, are forced to retire before they need to and before they want to, because corporations claim they're "rearranging" when really they're just getting rid of anyone over about 55. They'd much rather hire someone younger, who earns less and has fewer vacation days. I had worked for the same corporation for almost 20 years, and then one day I was just called into the office and told my job was ending. And my first response was, "What do you mean, ending?" All of a sudden, you're not part of the team anymore, and I've seen that happen to so many people before me and after me. I was really shocked and speechless, but I walked right down to the personnel office to find out about my severance package, and then I took my anger and resentment and turned them into fuel for finding another job, one that I enjoyed so much more. And the funny thing is, two weeks later, after I had been hired at my new job but was still finishing up at the old job, my boss called me and said they had decided they really did need someone to do my job, and asked if I still wanted to work. And I said, "You bet I want to work, but not for you. I've already taken another job."

—*VI HOWG*
MINNETONKA, MINNESOTA
YEARS RETIRED: 5

A GREAT FRIEND OF MINE SAID TO ME, "Just say yes to every invitation." Doesn't matter what it is—could be a dinner invitation or to participate in a session in the city or take classes. After some point in time you'll realize that you've said yes too many times, and you start to restructure. It's some of the best advice I've ever received.

—*FRED TEACH*
CANDLER, NORTH CAROLINA
YEARS RETIRED: 3

ASK THE COACH
CHANGE-UP: LEARNING TO DEAL WITH WHATEVER HAPPENS

When life throws me a curve ball, what is the first thing I should do?

The first thing to do is breathe! It sounds simple and like a silly thing to do. It's not. Curve balls—whether divorce, job loss or milder complications—have come at us, are coming at us and will come at us over the course of our lives. First, take a moment to ask yourself: How have I handled curve balls before? Have I tended to overreact? Have I been appropriately concerned but reasonable? Have I ignored warning signs for too long? Remind yourself and help yourself by understanding your history with curve balls and begin to create a plan of action based on that self-understanding.

How do I get comfortable with the prospect of big change?

Most of us experience change as "hitting the wall." The wall always wins and we end up bruised and battered, and still have to figure out how to get through it. Try to look at change as something that happens in cycles, like waves. Remember that change has happened before and will happen again. If you can, accept that change may in fact be your constant companion through life. Make friends with change by understanding what skills and resources you need to best work with (not against) it. You'll likely find yourself a lot more comfortable with the reality of change.

I'm living on my own. How can I gain self-confidence and feel OK about it?

If you are not comfortable being independent, or if you know that you are really ready for a partnership with another and that living on your own has become just plain lonely, don't despair. There are a couple of really constructive things you can do. Begin by recognizing what your "next best thing" might be. For example, if you don't want to have the weekend loom in front of you without concrete plans, then make some plans. Perhaps something better will come along and you will have to forgo your plan. But have what I call anchors in your weekend—plans with others, plans to attend events, plans to take your dog to the dog park or plans to volunteer at a shelter—and schedule these in advance. Don't wait for life to come to you.   On the flip side, find activities or places that make you feel comfortable being with yourself (notice I did not say *alone*). If you think about it, there is one person you are with from the moment you are born, 24/7, until your last moment—that is you. Why not make sure you treat yourself as you would your best friend?

What is the most important tip you'd give someone about starting over?

Be sure to have closure with whatever chapter you are ending. Recognize what you will miss and acknowledge it. Think about how you will want to add that back in at the appropriate time. Think about what lessons you've learned and what you won't repeat; be alert to this step because as you know, many of us repeat past mistakes. Once you've experienced closure, then you are ready to begin creating your next chapter—not starting over, but adding on to your life story.

Is there a positive opportunity in having to go through a challenging or difficult life change?

If you read about the world's greatest leaders and thinkers you will see that they all share something in common—the challenges associated with great change. I would argue that change is a prerequisite to a fulfilled life. Look at spiritual leaders: Moses, Jesus, Buddha. Look at political leaders: Lincoln, Roosevelt, Mandela. Look at inspirational leaders: Helen Keller, Stephen Hawking, Mother Theresa. Do you get the point? Life is a series of experiences; some good, some bad, some worse than that. The question is, which experiences will define you?

—B.W.

I WAS A BIOLOGY TEACHER AT OUR LOCAL HIGH SCHOOL.
In retirement, I am a professional writer. I was always
interested in writing, and I finally became so determined to be published that I submitted letters to
the editor, contributed to my church newsletter
and to anyone else who would accept my items!

> —JoAnn
> Joppa, Maryland
> Years retired: 9

• • • • • • • •

MY SCHOOL DISTRICT AUTOMATICALLY PUTS ITS RETIRED
Teachers into "super sub" status. This means that for one day
of substitute teaching, I make $140 as opposed to $80.
If you're a retired teacher, subbing is the perfect part-time
job because it pays well, it's flexible, and you get to keep in
touch with old colleagues and friends.

> —Kathy
> Washington, D.C.
> Years retired: 1

• • • • • • • •

I WAS QUITE FOCUSED ON MY WORK. It was and still is difficult
for me to realize that I am no longer in the mainstream of science. But I found something that is worthwhile to me. I'm the
executive editor of a journal entitled *Progress in Lipid
Research*. It is an international review journal. My job is to
invite established scientists from around the world to write
reviews on topics as they relate to the general field of lipids.

> —Howard Sprecher
> Columbus, Ohio
> Years retired: 5

• • • • • • • •

IN RETIREMENT, I'VE GOT A BUSINESS WITH MY HUSBAND. The
work we're doing now is a blessing in our lives. Our joy is
doing it together and going out on our little trips. Along the
way, we go for a bike ride or go for a picnic. It gives me joy.

> —Anonymous
> St. Paul, Minnesota

I OPENED MY OWN COMPUTER BUSINESS. It allowed me to meet new people and use my computer skills to help others. Otherwise, I would have been lonely sitting at home without a purpose to my days. It also meant I wasn't depending on my husband for petty cash. I believe women should always be self-reliant, even when retired.

—*SUSAN FUSS*
TORONTO, ONTARIO, CANADA
YEARS RETIRED: 5

THE BIGGEST CHALLENGES

One of the real challenges of retirement is planning wisely for new outlets to develop social networks and friendships during these years.

Health and the cost of not having health insurance emerged as the biggest issue, emotionally and financially, as people contemplate retirement.

I HAVE A PART-TIME JOB AS A JUDGE for the Democratic Party. Basically, I'm a judge at a polling location at every election, local and national. I've been doing this for six years and enjoy it, although it's more like volunteering because the pay is minimal!

—*M.A.R.*
DURHAM, NORTH CAROLINA
YEARS RETIRED: 8

I'M A REALLY BIG BASEBALL FAN, and when I started easing out of my day job, I applied and was hired for a position as a concierge host for the Seattle Mariners. It's been a real delight. I get to meet people, see baseball games for free, and still get paid.

—*HAROLD JAFFE*
REDMOND, WASHINGTON
YEARS RETIRED: 2

WHAT'S IN A WORD?

HAVE YOU NOTICED that all the synonyms for "retire" are depressing?

> —*ANONYMOUS*
> *CALIFORNIA*

• • • • • • • •

WHAT'S A BETTER TERM THAN SENIOR CITIZEN? Active Retiree. I've got that on my business card. That's the way I look at who I am now.

> —*FRED TEACH*
> *CANDLER, NORTH CAROLINA*
> *YEARS RETIRED: 3*

• • • • • • • •

WHAT'S A BETTER NAME for senior citizens? How about elders?

> —*B.D.*
> *SEATTLE, WASHINGTON*
> *YEARS RETIRED: 18*

• • • • • • • •

I DON'T BELIEVE IN THE WORD RETIRE. I've learned that once we stop having interests and helping people, we slowly die. It's so important for us to have something to get up for every morning. We have a choice of what we would like to do, but if we aren't doing something that is meaningful, our life ceases.

> —*MARY LOU COOK*
> *SANTA FE, NEW MEXICO*

• • • • • • • •

THE WORD "RETIREMENT" always seemed so stupid to me. You graduate to doing nothing? You can't play all the time. You can't travel all the time. Even having children and grandchildren is a nice hobby, and I enjoy it, but it's not a job.

> —*SUE SIEGAL*
> *SAN FRANCISCO, CALIFORNIA*

MY WIFE AND I HAD BOTH BEEN IN EDUCATION, so it seemed
natural we would go in that direction with our volunteer work.
We set up a Dollars for Scholars program, providing educational opportunities for children. Since we started the program, we have raised more than a million dollars in scholar-
ships for our community. Because my wife and I are such firm
believers in education and it's been instilled in us, if we can
help somebody else's child get an education, that
gives us a nice, warm feeling. I started kindergarten
back in the 1930s, and now in 2005, I'm still
involved in education.

—*B.L.*
CENTRALIA, WASHINGTON
YEARS RETIRED: 13

MORE CONTROL MEANS A LOT

According to both pre-retirees and retirees, the
best thing about retirement is having more control
over their time. One in three retirees said doing more
meaningful or satisfying work in retirement was
"very important."

I LOVE TO SOLVE PROBLEMS, and I was always interested in
computers. When I retired, I thought it would be fun to write
software programs for network administrators, so I started my
own business. It feels good to help solve problems. For example, computer users in school systems are constantly changing
due to changes in enrollment. I created software that automatically removes students from the network when they leave
school. It feels good to know that I've made someone's life
easier. There's also a nice feeling that comes with success.

—*JAMES EVANS*
REPUBLIC, MISSOURI
YEARS RETIRED: 5

WORKING LONGER: A REALITY CHECK

Myth: Given the growing retirement income challenge, people will have to work forever.
Reality: If individuals worked full time until at least 66, they could enjoy a long and financially secure retirement, with incomes one-third higher than if they retired at 62.

Myth: Older workers will choose to work longer on their own.
Reality: Most people retire as soon as benefits are available at age 62.

Myth: As baby boomers approach retirement, employers will embrace older workers.
Reality: Many employers are lukewarm toward retaining older workers due to concerns that they cost too much, lack current skills and don't plan to stick around long.

Myth: Employers will quickly change their tune in response to labor shortages.
Reality: Many employers with a high proportion of older workers are in declining industries. Others can tap global labor markets.

Myth: Older workers have little to offer employers.
Reality: Older workers often have advantages over younger workers, including higher productivity, better judgment, a stronger work ethic and better people skills.

Myth: Phased retirement—shifting to part-time employment with a career employer—is the solution for keeping people in the workforce longer.
Reality: Many firms are reluctant to offer phased retirement due to concerns over which workers would be eligible, health insurance costs and part-time schedules.

Myth: Most workers can work longer by remaining with their career employer.
Reality: Career employment is declining fast: Only 44% of male workers age 58-62 are still with their age-50 employer, down from 70% two decades ago.

Myth: The working longer prescription is the answer for everyone.
Reality: While today's older workers are generally healthier and better educated, up to a third could be hard pressed to work into their mid-60s due to poor health or job prospects.

Myth: Government cannot do much to encourage longer work lives.
Reality: Raising Social Security's earliest eligibility age of 62 could push back the work/retirement divide by changing the mindset of both workers and employers.

Myth: Eliminating mandatory retirement removed a major barrier to working longer.
Reality: Mandatory retirement could actually promote longer work lives by providing both employers and workers clear expectations about when careers end.

I'VE BEEN RETIRED FROM THE UTILITY COMPANY FIVE YEARS, but I've had my own classic car company on the side about 15 years. I started it on a lark and really got into it. It's kind of mushrooming and doing well, and now we're refurbishing classic cars and selling them around the world. It's just really fun, and I can make some money at it. And it's the kind of thing, if you want to devote more time to it, you can; if you want to devote less time to it, you can.

> —*CHALMERS GABLE*
> *MARION, TEXAS*
> *YEARS RETIRED: 5*

* * * * * * * *

RETIREMENT CAN BE A LOT LIKE FALLING OFF A CLIFF. One day you are fully occupied, and the next day you are wondering what to do. I think you have to retire slowly and gracefully. I still work part time so I won't have to fall off a cliff.

> —*YITZ*
> *MANCHESTER, UNITED KINGDOM*
> *YEARS RETIRED: 8*

* * * * * * * *

MY PENSION AND SOCIAL SECURITY have been almost enough, but I am not one to feel secure without a little savings. I like to keep some extra money coming in somehow. This is a good idea for anyone looking to retire: to have a skill you can use once in a while to keep you busy, make you feel useful, help your bank account a little. I do some home nursing every now and then, stay with a new mother for a few days, that kind of thing. I have one friend who got a real estate license, and her husband got a broker's license, and she helps her friends and their children with real estate—not as a full-time thing, just every now and again. She enjoys it.

> —*BETTY*
> *DURHAM, NORTH CAROLINA*
> *YEARS RETIRED: 8*

OPPORTUNITY CALLING

I HAD BEEN A WRITER, JOURNALIST and radio personality
in earlier years. When I got to be over 60, I wasn't as
interested in having a lot of work. I had other things I
wanted to do: staying in shape, skiing and building things.
At one point, I had an idea to do oral histories for people
for their families and for organizations. I started out
recording my girlfriend's father, who was 94 at the time.
I hadn't thought I would do it as a business, but it was so
successful and so liked by the family, I thought maybe I'd
do that for other people. Next, I did one for my ex-wife's
family for her father. And that got universal acclaim. So I
thought, "I'll start a little business." The idea is, at some
point down the road, a great-grandchild who has never
met his great-grandmother will want to know about her
life. And it will be there on a CD, in the great-grandmother's words and in her own voice. I love doing
this. I interviewed something like 10,000 people
in my working life, but this is as much fun as
I've ever had.

—*MICHAEL CREEDMAN*
SAN FRANCISCO, CALIFORNIA

MY ADVICE FOR A SUCCESSFUL RETIREMENT CONSISTS of three
essential things: First, stay intellectually active. Keep your
mind working. It doesn't matter what you're working on; it
needs to keep working. Second, remain physically active. I
ride my bike to work—13 miles—as often as I can. It's a fair
workout. And third, have future plans. I'm leaving in a week
for the Philippines, and then I'm going to China to visit my
daughter and her family. That's one of the essentials: not necessarily knowing what you'll do tomorrow, but having an idea
that next year maybe I'm going to be doing this, and in three
years I'll be doing that.

—*ROBERT L. ZIMDAHL*
FORT COLLINS, COLORADO
YEARS RETIRED: 1

THE BEST THING ABOUT RETIREMENT

WE HAVE TWO GRANDKIDS (8 AND 10), and we get to spend more time with them. Sometimes we keep the kids while my daughter is working. We have a lot of fun with them, especially at those ages. And I also do more things with my own kids than I did when I was working. For example, my daughter bought an old house, and I helped fix that up.

—*CHALMERS GABLE*
MARION, TEXAS
YEARS RETIRED: 5

• • • • • • • •

GETTING TO SLEEP THE HOURS YOU WANT TO SLEEP, and doing what you want to do, when you want to do it. That sounds kind of selfish, but when you work for 34 years and you have to be somewhere and on someone else's time, eat on their schedule, rush off to work, and then come home and constantly think about what you didn't get finished at work … well, being on your own clock and not someone else's is just the best!

—*HARRIET SMITH*
SAN ANTONIO, TEXAS
YEARS RETIRED: 2

• • • • • • • •

LIVING NEAR family members.

—*SAM KOSTICK*
SEATTLE, WASHINGTON
YEARS RETIRED: 4

I'M 93 NOW, AND I RETIRED at the end of the academic year of 1982. But I still go to the university two to five days a week, doing things that they ask me to do. Sometimes they ask me to do something I don't want to do, and I say no. Remain active in things you like to do. That doesn't mean you have to do them all the time. Just enough to keep you occupied. And stay in close touch with people. The interaction with others is important. Even if they're always complaining, that's better than nothing!

—*FRANCES LOMAS FELDMAN*
PASADENA, CALIFORNIA
YEARS RETIRED: 24

- - - - - - - - -

THE WELL-PREPARED

Among both pre-retirees and retirees, staying healthy and spending more time with family topped the list of priorities in retirement.

The study revealed, however, that only about half are doing any serious planning and preparation to make these priorities a reality.

- - - - - - - - -

SINCE RETIRING, I'VE UNDERGONE a drastic values clarification. I didn't realize how much of my life had been spent "majoring in the minors" until I was no longer working. Now, I have a new sense of time and a realization that life isn't infinite. Consequently, before committing to any activity, I strongly consider if it's worth my time. For example, I love to volunteer. But I used to run around like a chicken with her head cut off, trying to attend every single volunteer meeting because I felt I should be there. Now, I skip most of the meetings but contribute 120 percent to individual projects I feel are worthwhile. Life is so much more meaningful now.

—*GAY*
DENVER, COLORADO

VOLUNTEERING IS THE FASTEST WAY you can make new friends. I used to rely to a large extent on my wife's volunteer activities and the people she met. Now, in volunteering after retirement, I've met all sorts of people. It's a key way of getting to know people and the community.

—*BARRY MUNDT*
ASHEVILLE, NORTH CAROLINA
YEARS RETIRED: 14

I GOT VERY INVOLVED WITH THE American Association of University Women, I joined the board of I Love a Parade, which helps homeless people to find work through the arts, and I regularly visit nursing homes with an elderly woman from church. I also serve on the environmental action team at church, I coordinate the art exhibits there, and I've been in charge of the rummage sale for the past three years. I enjoy the things I do, but I am trying to be careful to restrict myself to certain things and not take on others. I'm working very hard to create downtime.

—*CYNTHIA*
ST. PAUL, MINNESOTA
YEARS RETIRED: 8

YOU CAN'T JUST QUIT AND SIT IN A CHAIR NOW. You'd go nuts or eat bonbons and blow up and die or something. You have to do something. Don't isolate yourself!

—*ALLAN S. ROSS*
SAN ANTONIO, TEXAS
YEARS RETIRED: 1

REMEMBER, YOU ARE A VALUABLE CITIZEN whether you work or not.

—*GEORGE RIES*
SEATTLE, WASHINGTON
YEARS RETIRED: 30

IT'S NOT A GOOD IDEA TO RETIRE COLD TURKEY. I did, and at first I thought it was great not having to get up in the morning. I'd roll out of bed at 11 a.m. and spend the day leisurely browsing around Barnes & Noble. After about a month, the excitement wore off, and I began to miss the daily challenge and stress of my job. For that reason, I'm currently putting in an application for an assistant principalship. Some of us just weren't meant to stop working, I guess.

—*JEFFREY WACO*
NEW YORK, NEW YORK
YEARS RETIRED: 2

* * * * * * * *

I'M IN A SORT OF COMPROMISE WITH RETIREMENT: I'm almost 68, and I'm working at the library as a staff writer four days a week. This means I still have the satisfaction of work and more free time at the same time. It gives me the amazing gift of three-day weekends, which, after four years, is still a pure delight. By Friday evening, I sometimes think it's Saturday, and I still have a weekend. Then by Sunday evening, I'm ready to go back to work.

—*SUE*
PHILADELPHIA, PENNSYLVANIA
YEARS RETIRED: 1

* * * * * * * *

TO SOME, RETIREMENT MEANS THAT YOU STOP WORKING. But if you love what you're doing, retirement is more about finding ways to do the same thing on your own terms. The secret to retirement for me has been to find ways to keep teaching without having to get up every single morning at 4:50 a.m., and without having to go to work every single day. I love days off here and there, but my eyes cloud over when I don't have something to plan for.

—*JAMES MAHONEY*
YARDLEY, PENNSYLVANIA
YEARS RETIRED: 8

GIVE YOURSELF A FEW MONTHS AFTER retirement before you think about part-time work (if you have to think about it); plan fun activities for those first few months. As I worked on my finances, I came up with a plan that will let me be comfortable after 10 years of retirement. In the meantime, I will have to work part-time to enjoy the things I want to do. The plan is to think about combining my other interests with paying jobs. Among the considerations: working in a garden center during the heaviest season; working in a ski resort so that I can improve my skiing; becoming a "temp" so that I can experience a lot of new job situations and people; volunteering in national parks (room and board is free, but no salary); marketing my photos at crafts fairs or other venues.

—*PHIL MACKALL*
ARLINGTON, VIRGINIA
YEARS RETIRED: 1

I DECIDED WHEN I WAS 60 that I'd probably work for another 10 years. The decision point was: Do I want to keep doing what I was doing for another 10 years, or do I want to do something different for the next 10 years? It wasn't something I could put off. If I was ever going to do something different, now was the time. I was in a fortunate position because I happened to be married to someone who was still bringing in a paycheck. I wouldn't have made this decision if I still had younger children or was single.

—*PAULA*
VANCOUVER, B.C., CANADA
YEARS RETIRED: 3

I WAS LOOKING FOR AN INVESTMENT that would bring in some extra money but not require a lot of time to run. I found a storage business for sale near our lake home. My wife and I agreed to buy it. It is very low maintenance. I have to mow it during the summer months, but that is about it. This is a growing area, so I don't have trouble finding renters. I get one or two who don't want to pay their rent, but overall everyone is good about mailing me their payments. It's the perfect business!

> —*J.L.*
> *CLIMAX SPRINGS, MISSOURI*
> *YEARS RETIRED: 10*

• • • • • • • •

AFTER A LIFE OF TEACHING, I thought I would retire and never want to set foot in a classroom again. But after a few years, I became friendly with some new neighbors and started tutoring their little girl. It was such a different experience than being a teacher; doing it because I wanted to help, rather than as a job, made it incredibly rewarding when that girl's math grade went from a C- to a B+. So I decided to tutor in the local school. The kids are so grateful.

> —*FRANK*
> *CHARLESTON, SOUTH CAROLINA*
> *YEARS RETIRED: 5*

• • • • • • • •

WHEN I WAS WORKING I RODE WHAT I CALLED MY BOAT. I rode it pretty well. I'm a strong guy and I take good strokes and propelled my boat rather rapidly. But now, in my involvement with the industry, I am still in my boat but I take short strokes and I sort of glide and watch the world. It's worked out to be quite enjoyable. Now I just go with what motivates me at the time. It meets my needs at this stage in life. I went from 135 employees to one—me.

> — *BOB WALDORF*
> *LOS ANGELES, CALIFORNIA*
> *YEARS RETIRED: 11*

I'M INVOLVED IN THE **AARP TAX-AIDE PROGRAM,** which provides tax preparation help to seniors and low-income people. I didn't have any particular experience in tax preparation—just doing my own—but I've always liked math and have a knack for it. Volunteers get five days of training, and then they can pick the site they'd like to work at. I work two afternoons a week, and we help about 30 people a day. When you get someone with a very low income, and you can get as much as $3,000 back for them, you just feel good.

—*MARY ANNE PAGE*
MINNEAPOLIS, MINNESOTA

• • • • • • • •

I ALWAYS TELL MY GIRLFRIENDS THAT IT'S **OK** for people our age to work, but they shouldn't be working at McDonald's. Nobody looks good in those uniforms, but especially not people of our age.

—*ANN MARIE BUSH*
POLAND, OHIO

• • • • • • • •

START A BUSINESS. I know that many start-up businesses fail, but I didn't have the income pressures that so many people do when they're just beginning a business. I was able to treat my new career as a hobby that got out of hand. I'm earning money now and my business is growing slowly, but I don't have to tear out my hair and starve in order to get it going.

—*J.S.*
SCOTCH PLAINS, NEW JERSEY
YEARS RETIRED: 4

• • • • • • • •

I'M TAKING A COURSE AT **NYU** ON FILM. I'm a movie buff. It's a continuing-ed course called "Movies 101." It's taught by the film professor Richard Brown. They screen a film, then they have actors there to talk about the film. It was pricey, but I really wanted to do it, and I knew I could give up something else.

—*JOAN ALAGNA*
BROOKLYN, NEW YORK
YEARS RETIRED: 2

I'M ALWAYS SO AMAZED at the seniors I meet who are afraid
of new situations. Fear is the silent killer of seniors!

> —*BEVERLY*
> *ATLANTA, GEORGIA*
> *YEARS RETIRED: 4*

· · · · · · · ·

YOU HAVE TO LEARN TO SAY NO AND ONLY DO THE THINGS
that you want and/or need to do. Retired people need to be
assertive about finding activities within their abilities. Then
they need to be generous with their skills and time, positive
... and no whining!

> —*ANONYMOUS*
> *NEVADA*
> *YEARS RETIRED: 13*

· · · · · · · ·

THOUGH I AM SOMEWHAT RETIRED PROFESSIONALLY (at least
slowed down), I am not in a retirement mode emotionally or
intellectually, and I have actually been giving seminars on
helping people prepare for retirement. As a psychiatric social
worker, I try to help people look inside themselves in order to
explore and express their deepest interest. It is not always
easy, but very gratifying.

> —*BEVERLY ZEIDENBERG*
> *BETHESDA, MARYLAND*
> *YEARS RETIRED: 2*

· · · · · · · ·

I STAY ACTIVE WITH MY PART-TIME JOBS. And I tell my wife it's
a good way to meet girls.

> —*JAMES SALTER*
> *YOUNGSTOWN, OHIO*

· · · · · · · ·

SOME PEOPLE WOULD BE ONLY too pleased to work 10 hours
a week in retirement. Other people require a great deal
more. I'm one of those people; I don't do things half finished.

> —*ART KOFF*
> *CHICAGO, ILLINOIS*
> *YEARS RETIRED: 8*

RETIRED PEOPLE ARE A HUGE LABOR FORCE in the volunteer world. If they're able, it's better for them to utilize their skills and interests. Everyone should contribute while he or she can. In doing so, you'll feel better about yourself and stay even healthier. Plus, the structure helps.

—*DEB CARLSON KLAIN*
CLEVELAND, OHIO

* * * * * * * *

IF YOU HAD TOLD ME HOW MUCH ENJOYMENT A PERSON could get out of doing something and not getting paid for it, I would not have believed you. I spent most of my life on the fast track, trying to advance career-wise and make as much money as I possibly could. If it didn't pay, I had no interest in it. But my wife has been involved in many organizations, and she guilted me into spending some time with her at our library. I fussed about it at first, but now I can't spend enough time there. I especially enjoy time in the children's area and watching the fun and excitement of the little ones as they pick out a book that they get to take home. I feel guilty, most days, because I get more out of it than I give.

—*DAVID FELZKE*
MORGANTOWN, WEST VIRGINIA
YEARS RETIRED: 5

* * * * * * * *

I DON'T BELIEVE YOU SHOULD PROFIT from our capitalist society and not give back to those who need it. After I retired, I joined an international program through my church that sent us to Ecuador to help with children and education there. It wasn't so much hands-on as it was using my business experience to set up systems that would help people. It was extremely rewarding. And it was a beautiful part of the world. Give back. You finally have the time to do it; just do it.

—*E.R.*
TAMPA, FLORIDA
YEARS RETIRED: 10

I WORK WITH THE DRAMATICS GROUP, which produces a play-reading once a month. I sometimes act or direct and always edit the videos of the productions. I'm interested in every aspect of the theater, and I like to act.

—SAM KOSTICK
SEATTLE, WASHINGTON
YEARS RETIRED: 4

* * * * * * * *

THINK ABOUT DOING SOMETHING COMPLETELY DIFFERENT.
My wife retired from the university and started a mediation business, which is what she had done in her career. But she's also starting an orchid business. She loves gardening and orchids and became good at growing and taking care of them. She said, "Let's try a little business thing and sell them." She likes it very much.

—EUGENE C. BIANCHI
ATHENS, GEORGIA
YEARS RETIRED: 5

* * * * * * * *

RETIREMENT IS A BIG ADJUSTMENT. You can't work at a job for 40-some years, and one Monday just not go in to work! Make sure you will have enough things to keep you busy. I had a hard time adjusting and almost made my wife crazy because I didn't do nearly enough. But over time I've come up with routines and things to do to fill my days.

—JOHN R. BRIGHT
ALLENTOWN, PENNSYLVANIA
YEARS RETIRED: 10

* * * * * * * *

VOLUNTEERING IS WITHOUT A DOUBT my single favorite activity. I work with a variety of groups, doing publicity for one, serving on the board of another, helping organize an auction for another, and so on. The variety of activities and the opportunity to make lots of new acquaintances and friends is wonderful.

—SUSAN
TAYLOR, TEXAS
YEARS RETIRED: 3

WHEN I RETIRED, I started thinking about getting a part-time job. A friend who was a manager of a local credit union said, "We may have a job for you." So they hired me. My younger daughter couldn't believe it. She said, "Dad, you only have a three-day retirement?" It just seemed like the right thing, and so that's what I did. I kept working for them for eight years.

—*B.L.*
CENTRALIA, WASHINGTON
YEARS RETIRED: 13

• • • • • • • •

WORKING SINCE MY RETIREMENT HAS OPENED UP a whole new world to me that I knew virtually nothing about. I have been working as a part-time librarian, and it has been wonderful. My friend who works at the library suggested I give it a try, but I had no experience doing that kind of work. I've been learning as I go. I love it. I actually look forward to it each morning. If you are going to work after you retire, you might as well try something different.

—*MITCH TERRIS*
BOARDMAN, OHIO

• • • • • • • •

I DIDN'T PLAN ON WORKING AGAIN FULL TIME, but I'm back in the swing of things. I'm teaching psychology classes at a community college: six courses, 16 classes a week! I was working part time, but the head of the psychology department got a promotion and asked me to take on extra classes for her. It's really interesting work.

—*DONNA RICH*
CHARLOTTE, NORTH CAROLINA
YEARS RETIRED: 4

• • • • • • • •

RETIREMENT IS A RECENT MAN-MADE IDEA. It's not natural. You think the pioneers retired when they reached a certain age? It's just not the way things are supposed to be. We were made to work.

—*GREG DEVRIES*
POLAND, OHIO

THE OLDER I GET, the shorter my CV becomes. The reason is that I think I can distinguish the important from the unimportant. The word "retirement" has an implication of withdrawing from action: I think that's a misconception. And if I looked at retirement like that I'd be scared to retire, too.

—*PETER L. THIGPEN*
KENTFIELD, CALIFORNIA

I WORKED FOR OVER 40 YEARS in the school system. Change for me doesn't come naturally but the idea of change is very exciting. I just retired: I think, why did I do this, I love my work, and I keep reminding myself that change is exhilarating and let's go find that dream. It's a time of self-exploration; it's a process. What do you need to do to make a change?

—*SYLVIA BROWN*
VALLEY VILLAGE, CALIFORNIA
YEARS RETIRED: LESS THAN 1

IF I WANTED TO RUN A MARATHON I CERTAINLY COULD. There is nobody out there who is going to say, "You're 65! You shouldn't be running a marathon." Now it's my choice. There was a much greater sense of conformity 50 years ago. People conformed to those shoulds and shouldn'ts. People toed the line; people did the expected and followed the norm. Well, what's the norm now?

—*BERYN HAMMIL*
SAN FRANCISCO BAY AREA, CALIFORNIA

I DON'T THINK OF MYSELF AS RETIRED because I'm still spending a good portion of my time either trying to make money or making money. When you are self-employed you spend a lot of time marketing yourself and networking, and that's work— that's not just hanging out.

—*PAULA*
VANCOUVER, B.C., CANADA
YEARS RETIRED: 3

IT'S ABOUT TIME PEOPLE STARTED getting on the bandwagon and seeing age as a good thing. In other countries they do. People lie about their age in other countries. They don't say they are younger; they say they're older.

      —*CINDY JOSEPH*
        NEW YORK, NEW YORK

• • • • • • • •

IF YOU WANT TO SIT ON A BENCH in a park there are plenty of benches. I could sit on a bench in the sun and slowly see my brain turn to oatmeal.

      —*MORT SHEINMAN*
        NEW YORK, NEW YORK
        YEARS RETIRED: 10

• • • • • • • •

I FIGURED 46 YEARS OF WORK WAS ENOUGH FOR ONE LIFETIME. I wanted to see what else I could do with my time. What I wanted to do more than anything else was tend to my garden. That's my real passion. I wish I could have gotten paid to do that. Now I tell people I'm a full-time gardener working for the best boss in the world—me.

      —*P.Y.*
        BARRELVILLE, MARYLAND
        YEARS RETIRED: 4

The Possible Dream: Living with Purpose and Passion

It's ironic, really: Retirement is a concept so many of us look forward to, but when it arrives, it creates a space many of us don't know, right away, how to fill. Taking time to go on vacation and explore the country or the world, playing golf or simply not having a work schedule to follow is often enough … for the first couple of years. After that, people typically feel ready for something more. For some, knowing what their passion is and how to repurpose themselves comes easily. In this chapter you will hear from people who took the skills and capabilities they developed over years of working for pay and now use those same skills to give back to organizations that can't afford to pay them. It benefits the organization tremendously to have highly competent volunteer staff and it enables "protirees" to share their gifts without the stress of being ultimately responsible for the organization. When the day is over, they close their computers and go off to their next meaningful activity!

Others find their passion lies in a love of sports, of art or of music. Many people revisit long-buried dreams about taking classes to develop their skills. You'll read about people who become bakers, *artists or students. They are living proof that retirement is the perfect opportunity to explore the creative side of your passionate self.*

As we age, the idea of making a contribution takes on more and more importance. That sense of legacy, of contributing to the betterment of your community or the world, is now a distinct possibility. You will read about people who have paid attention while traveling and developed programs in other countries to address a need that wasn't being met. Others work closer to home, volunteering with youth, arts organizations and libraries, and on nonprofit boards of directors.

The opportunities to contribute are there once you discover what you feel passionate about and how you would like to spend your time.

TODAY I AM WORKING WITH youth as they complete court-mandated community service. Many come back to volunteer with me long after their mandates are complete. I've met a ton of government officials, mayors, governors, senators, etc. But the most memorable are those who are helped and come back and tell me they would like to help others. I have volunteers with me today who were once guests at a soup kitchen I have volunteered at for about nine years. I found my volunteer connections through the JPMorgan Chase Foundation. And I continue to work with Chase employees long after I have retired.

—*MAUREEN O'BOYLE*
NEW YORK, NEW YORK
YEARS RETIRED: 6

• • • • • • • • •

I DON'T MISS WORK AS MUCH AS I thought I would. I was a practicing nurse for nearly 40 years, and it became such a large and integral part of my life. I thought I'd have to find a new identity. But after about a month of retirement, I found that I didn't really need to work to find fulfillment in my life. I've found just as much contentment by spending time with my family and friends.

—*J.E.*
MORGANTOWN, WEST VIRGINIA
YEARS RETIRED: 2

• • • • • • • • •

HAVING SPENT SO MUCH OF MY TIME WORKING, I had never done any volunteering. I went to the website www.volunteer-match.org and ended up responding to requests for volunteers to about 12-14 different organizations (I never received a response from the majority of them). I had heard that because of the economy, there was a flood of volunteering so that individuals could show a continuous work history instead of a break in employment. Also because of the economy, I found that a part-time job was not much of a reality.

—*CECELIA WRAY*
ATLANTA, GEORGIA
YEARS RETIRED: LESS THAN 1

THE COACH'S CORNER

VOLUNTEER, AND MAKE YOURSELF HAPPY

Here's a little secret that only the happiest among us know: When we offer our time and ourselves we inevitably reap much more than we give.

Volunteering is a powerful way to engage in activities that have tremendous benefits to society while also yielding a sense of personal legacy that is increasingly important to so many of us. A recent survey suggests that people age 50 and over want to find new opportunities that are important in two distinct ways: They must be personally satisfying and they must help to enhance quality of life in the community.

How likely is this to change the world as we know it? Highly likely, when we consider the fact that the number of Americans age 55 and over will exceed *100 million* in the next couple of decades. Never before have we had a population so highly educated and interested in putting their education and experience to good use.

Not surprisingly, there are more and more ways to volunteer. You can take a volunteering "vacation" that may involve traveling by caravan, working in national parks across the country and visiting exotic international locations.

Given the thousand of volunteer opportunities that exist, how do you begin to understand how to get involved and what questions should you ask? Use the following questions as a baseline and add your own to reflect your interests and experience:

- Is there a job description for this placement that identifies specific skills, required experience and desired outcomes?

- What is the time frame for this particular assignment?

- Does the organization invest in its volunteer program and if so, how? (Staffing? Space for volunteers to work?)

- Is it possible to develop a volunteer schedule that allows for my relatively frequent travel plans?

- Do you offer training and support for volunteers? Is there someone who will work with me and answer any questions I might have?

—B.W.

THE FIRST 30 DAYS OF RETIREMENT, you're on a vacation. The next 30 days, you're starting to get uncomfortable. You're twitching, trying to find something to do, like paint dresser drawers. The next 30 days, you find something to do, like taking a class or playing golf, something that amuses you. And finally, the next month, you think, "What would I do if I could do anything?" And, of course, you can do anything, so you go out and go for it.

—*FRANK HAWK*
LAKELAND, FLORIDA
YEARS RETIRED: 3

. . . .

ON NPR THEY SAID THAT 40 PERCENT of teachers who were baby boomers would be retiring and there would be a shortage of teachers. I said, that's me, I could do that. I could teach. I transitioned from being a telecommunications executive to being a high school history teacher. I was 55. I learned a lot working with those kids. The major difference between those kids and me is that I've never woken up a day in my life wondering if anybody loved me. These kids didn't wake up with the assurance that they were lovable. So I loved those kids.

—*TIM WILL*
RUTHERFORD COUNTY, NORTH CAROLINA
YEARS RETIRED: NOYB

IN MY VOLUNTEER WORK, I know without a shadow of a doubt that I don't want to be promoted, given more work, more responsibility, a bigger office, a bigger desk, a bigger title. I don't mind giving advice if asked at work, but I have zero desire to be the responsible party, the person-in-charge. At the end of the day, I close up my PC, clean up my desk, put my pencils and paper clips away, wish everyone a good night and walk away in the cold air, quite happy with myself. Ah, freedom!

> —*JUDY CAPEL*
> *NEW YORK, NEW YORK*
> *YEARS RETIRED: 3*

• • • • • • • •

WHEN I GROW UP

Volunteering is a great way to keep busy, use your new downtime for good, *and* enjoy activities and careers you didn't pursue the first time around. America has 1.5 million nonprofit organizations, and they all rely on the volunteer labor of the 65 million Americans who offer their time and efforts each year. The options don't stop there—consider that around 75% of our firefighters are volunteers! Now is your chance to get involved, and don't forget: This kind of fun won't cost you a penny.

• • • • • • • •

I PLAY SAXOPHONE AND CLARINET. When I retired I joined a local senior band. We play for elderly housing facilities, nursing homes and local events. It was great to play again and make new friends. I also play solos at church on occasion and play in another band in a small nearby village. I feel very fortunate to still be playing music at this point in life.

> —*JIM*
> *MORTON, ILLINOIS*
> *YEARS RETIRED: 17*

YOU DON'T RETIRE FROM SOMETHING; you retire *to* something.

> —*CHARLIE*
> *HARTSDALE, NEW YORK*
> *YEARS RETIRED: 14*

• • • • • • • •

WE'RE IN TERRIBLE ECONOMIC TIMES and all nonprofits are feeling the pinch. The Grant Writing Residency Program I codirect at ReServe takes excellent writers, puts them through training and pairs each with a nonprofit organization. And through that process, we hope to create professional grant writers. With my background and broad knowledge of journalists and writers, I became responsible for recruiting writers. We have found some extraordinarily good writers, some from *The New York Times* and some from other newspapers or magazines, and a few who didn't have a journalism background but were very able. The stipend is $10 an hour, which is psychologically good. Most are very happy with that they're doing.

> –*LINDA AMSTER*
> *NEW YORK, NEW YORK*
> *YEARS RETIRED: 5*

• • • • • • • •

WHATEVER IT IS YOU COULDN'T DO when you were working, do it now. The older you get, the more you realize that the old adage is true: Life is short. When you're physically and mentally able to do what you want to do, do it. Don't have regrets later.

> —*CHALMERS GABLE*
> *MARION, TEXAS*
> *YEARS RETIRED: 5*

• • • • • • • •

DON'T RUSH INTO NEW THINGS TOO QUICKLY. Relax and breathe deeply and see what comes bubbling up and has been hidden under the aura of business during your working years.

> —*EMILY KIMBALL*
> *RICHMOND, VIRGINIA*

**I WAS ALWAYS HANDY AND ALWAYS WANTED TO TRY SCULPT-
ING,** but I never felt like I had the time or the opportunity. It's
been an amazing experience for me, and I've created some
pieces that decorate our home. I've also continued to garden
as a hobby. I've always had a garden, and I practically grew
up on a farm, so this was important to me. My
wife and I moved to an apartment complex,
but the town has gardens that are leased for
the summer. I grow vegetables, and I'm
generally there a few times a week.

> —CHARLIE
> HARTSDALE, NEW YORK
> YEARS RETIRED: 14

AT NONPROFITS, I have not found people playing the corpo-
rate politics that I saw in for-profit businesses. I have not had
to worry about being "downsized." The people I work with,
both employees and volunteers, are more cooperative and
more focused on accomplishing the organizations' missions.
There's less stress; I enjoy life more.

> —FRANK PENNYPACKER
> SUN PRAIRIE, WISCONSIN
> YEARS RETIRED: 7

I'VE CREATED A LINE OF COSMETICS CALLED BOOM!. Instead of
anti-age, anti-wrinkle, anti-this, it's pro-age, pro-women, pro-
natural-beauty. Isn't that great?

> —CINDY JOSEPH
> NEW YORK, NEW YORK

ONE OF MY FIELDS OF EXPERTISE IN CRIMINAL INVESTIGATION
was composite art drawing. Also, over the years of writing
police reports, I discovered a love of putting words together.
So, from the first day of retirement I began to write short stories and do my own illustrations.

> —BILL STRAIN
> KERRVILLE, TEXAS
> YEARS RETIRED: 6

A SEMI-START-UP

IF I HANG AROUND THE HOUSE for a few hours, my wife says, "Don't you have someplace to go?" So I started thinking, "There's very little for the 50-plus and 60-plus age group on the Internet." Since I was involved heavily with the Internet in advertising, I decided to start RetiredBrains.com, as a job and information source for the 50-plus age group. We posted a great deal of information, including arthritis pain, diabetes, memory loss and continuing education. We got a substantial amount of our traffic from those content areas.

Now that many older Americans are finding they need more income—the funds have been depleted, the value of their homes is less, the cost of health care is more than anticipated—most of the traffic now comes to the Jobs and Start Your Own Business area. I also created a brochure with this content in it, and a few of my friends said I should do something in book form. So I sent it off to a number of publishers, and to my delight, almost all the major publishers contacted me and said, "Let's talk further about this." I ended up writing a reference guide for boomers and retirees called *Invent Your Retirement: Resources for the Good Life.*

When I started this, I didn't realize it would be as much work as it is. I was hoping to be semi-retired and I haven't been able to be semi-retired because of the book and the site. There are also a number of areas in opening a business that I have no background on. And so I started looking for partners, and I have found some to join me.

— *ART KOFF*
   CHICAGO, ILLINOIS
   YEARS RETIRED: 8

INTERNSHIPS FOR MIDDLE AND LATER LIFE: YOUR QUESTIONS ANSWERED

An internship at my age? Aren't internships for kids?
Sure, some of them are, but not all of them—and it's quite possible to remodel one you like to fit your needs, or to design an internship for yourself at an organization you like. Internships can be your foot in the door at the business of your choice.

Internships were originally intended for college students to get experience in the real world, and for companies to groom potential new hires. With changing times and the 50-and-over age group ballooning, internships are one of the best ways for both older workers and organizations to give each other a test run.

In student internships, it is the company that offers experience to young people. In internships for older workers, *we* offer the company *our* experience. What we get in return depends on why we chose that particular company or internship in the first place, and how we designed our internship to work. Internships most often require a higher task level than typical volunteer work. They're short-term, part-time and project-oriented—a perfect fit if you want to leave time to visit the grandkids, take a class and even squeeze in a summer vacation.

With advances in technology and the currently shaky global economy, there's a revolution going on in the work force. Lots of "traditional" jobs are gone: In their place are part-time and contract work opportunities. It's very expensive for a company to find someone with the temperament, interest and skills that best match their organization. When an experienced and savvy older person arrives, with a proven work ethic and a written internship proposal in hand, asking for short-term, *unpaid* work, many companies will jump at the opportunity.

How do I know what kind of internship I want? Do you want a plain job, or an offbeat adventure? Is there a compelling service or cause that you've never had time for until now? A fantasy you'd like to pursue?

Start by writing a note to yourself that begins: "I've always wanted to _____ ." Your blank space may read: work in an art gallery, open a bakery shop, work in Washington, help disadvantaged children. Continue to write about what you'd like to do, and be as specific as possible. It's a great way to discover what motivates you, what field you'd like to explore and where you'd like to offer your skills.

Are all internships unpaid? Usually they are, but not always. Depending on the job you do, you may be able to ask for compensation or name your hours, and eventually parlay your experience into a new project (or job) of your choice. Be sure to ask for regular mentoring and feedback as part of the "pay" you receive.

So where are these internships? Check the library or a bookstore and look at the dozens of catalogs offering internships. Almost all of the internships listed will be for students, but don't give up! Just like remodeling a house, the task is to remodel the internship to fit you. Follow the application procedure and steps suggested, but be sure to write a compelling cover letter that includes your background, why you're interested, the skills you're bringing to them, the reasons they should choose you and your resume. (include accent on both "e"s in resume.

The other way to snag an internship is to design one for yourself. Choose a company, person or organization you'd truly love to be associated with. Do your homework and find out what they need, then create a project for yourself where *you* are the answer to that need, and follow the steps above.

It sounds like a lot of work. It is, but it's worth it. It's much the same as applying for a job, but you're in charge and you're not limited to listed job openings. It's risk-free for both you and the company. Internships are designed around experience—either sharing or receiving it. In today's world, getting an experienced older worker, often for free or nearly free—even for a short time—is a bonus few organizations can afford to pass up. Sometimes an internship results in a paid job, but even if it doesn't, it can lead you to places you've only dreamed about.

—Julie Lopp
InternShop™
Santa Barbara, California

THINK ABOUT WHAT YOU'VE always admired someone else doing, and then do that. I know guys who have started with rudimentary carpentry and are now cabinetmakers. All of a sudden, you've got the time to do this.

    —WILLIAM WERWAISS
    NEW YORK, NEW YORK

• • • • • • • • •

I TAKE CLASSES IN BAKING. I always wanted to be a better cook when I was working. Now I bake for my family and friends. People really appreciate this, and it makes me feel good. Wish I had started sooner!

    —NELSON
    TEMPE, ARIZONA
    YEARS RETIRED: 5

YOU CAN STILL HAVE A DREAM

LAST YEAR I WENT TO A SYMPOSIUM FOR WOMEN. I can't tell you what the topic was, because after I heard what I heard, I didn't even zero in on the rest of it. The woman was talking and she said, "Can you still have a dream?"... and that sentence so resonated with me.

I did a lot of talking to myself: If I retired, what would I want to do? How do I see myself? How do I want to be seen? I decided that I like the idea of helping people, teaching something, and giving out information. I watched an interview with a woman from Harvard who talked about the last chapter of your life. And I thought, this would be a great thing, to have a symposium on the third chapter of your life. She couldn't come out, so I put together a three-program package, First, a discussion about the next 10 to 20 years of your life, which I would be leading, and my friend, who is a financial advisor, would talk about it from a financial point of view and then we got somebody to talk about health. We put it on and it was very successful. I plan to see if I can get other organizations to host it.

—SYLVIA BROWN
VALLEY VILLAGE, CALIFORNIA
YEARS RETIRED: LESS THAN 1

818-762-5511

ONE NIGHT I HAD A HEART "EVENT." After much testing, it was determined that I had atrial fibrillation and that it was caused by stress, probably from being retired. Strike One against retirement! The solution was to get a job and start working again. Fortunately I had a good friend at the Elmira/Corning Regional Airport. He convinced his boss that I would make a good PR person for the company. I was hired at a very low salary and no benefits—but hey, I was working again and my stress level decreased.

—BOB BELL
ELMIRA, NEW YORK
YEARS RETIRED: 15

- - - - - - - - -

START FRESH

Many Americans over 50 don't intend to stop working after retirement—in fact, a study shows that 76% of baby boomers plan on changing careers after "retiring" and continuing on as a part of the workforce. This time, however, many of these retirees are looking for something a little different, perhaps a dream deferred or a newfound passion. Whether bored with their current career or forced out of their previous job, a desire for change is evident: another study shows that of Americans between 50 and 70, 57% want to find meaning in their work, and 50% want their work to positively affect the world around them.

- - - - - - - - -

SLEEP LATE ONE WEEKDAY MORNING AND THINK, "Wow! What fun is this!"

—NOLA SMITH
TAMPA, FLORIDA
YEARS RETIRED: 25

DON'T WAIT UNTIL AFTER YOU RETIRE TO FIND A HOBBY. It's
not that easy to find something that you want to spend a lot
of time doing; it's trickier than it sounds. I have friends who
like to golf, but when they retired, they found that they didn't
want to do it every day. For me, it's gardening. I could spend
all day puttering around out there, and most days I do.

> —*ANONYMOUS*
> *EAST PALESTINE, OHIO*
> *YEARS RETIRED: 1*

ONCE YOU VOLUNTEER, you have to learn how to say no. You
have to decide what your priorities are. You don't want to
end up volunteering for 10 different things and find you have
no time for yourself.

> —*CAROL GILLEN*
> *ASHEVILLE, NORTH CAROLINA*
> *YEARS RETIRED: 9*

I BELONG TO THREE TENNIS LEAGUES, I play golf two times a
week, I belong to a reader's theater group, I sing with a
band, and last year I was in five plays. If you get hooked up
with a senior center, there's no limit to the amount of things
you can find to do.

> —*JANIS*
> *CARY, NORTH CAROLINA*
> *YEARS RETIRED: 8*

EIGHT OR NINE YEARS AGO I scratched my head and said,
"What am I going to do when I retire?" I'd always had an
interest in painting, so I went ahead and started taking classes. I don't consider myself a painter or an artist, but I've had
a couple of shows. I've sold a few pieces at a very modest
price from time to time. I like to be creative. It's important to
look forward and find meaning about this life of ours.
Painting is a new challenge for me.

> —*ROY CLARY*
> *BROOKLYN, NEW YORK*
> *YEARS RETIRED: 1*

A NEW LIFE

MY HUSBAND STEVE IS a radiation oncologist who had been practicing medicine. I had been a Special Ed teacher, and then a stay-at-home mom; I loved it. When our son Peter was killed on September 11, our whole world turned upside down. About six months later, Steve gradually started to unload his patients and retire— there was no way he could concentrate and continue to be the doctor that he was before. We knew we had to create our memorial. We are not going to rely on someone else to do that. You can see nothing is happening in downtown New York. We wanted to leave a mark that Peter existed. And we wanted the world to be a better place because Peter had lived. But we didn't have a clue what to do.

Then one night I saw a program on *Nightline* with Dr. Richard Mollica, who is one of the world experts in dealing with traumatized populations. I learned that there were one billion people who had experienced trauma, torture, or mass violence. Sixty percent suffered such severe traumatic depression and PTSD that they could no longer function. I realized there was nothing we could do for Pete but if in his name we could return people to life, then that was the very best thing we could do to honor him. I couldn't wait to wake Steve up the next morning and tell our other two kids. Ever since then we work seven days a week, 10 hours a day. This was in no way the direction that our lives had been going. For me, it's been a lifesaver — coming from a place where I never thought I would ever feel good again, I finally feel good about the work we are doing and the people we are helping and the people that we are meeting along the way. Our foundation has treated more than 100,000 patients.

—*LIZ ALDERMAN*
ROCHESTER COUNTY, NEW YORK
WWW.PETERCALDERMANFOUNDATION.ORG
YEARS RETIRED: 0

I WAS LOOKING FORWARD TO RETIREMENT until it actually happened. There was a sudden realization that I was entering a new phase of life. I was bored those first few weeks. That phase only lasted a short time, though. I slowly started doing projects around the house that I had been putting off. I also started exploring new things. I had always wanted to go off-roading in Colorado. I finally bought a Jeep and went. I can't imagine working now. All of my friends have gone through a similar phase. You just have to give it some time. Think of life as an adventure, and you will never run out of things to do.

> —J.L.
> CLIMAX SPRINGS, MISSOURI
> YEARS RETIRED: 10

. . . .

FIGURE OUT A WAY THAT YOUR HOBBY CAN HELP OTHERS. I like to knit, so I joined a group that meets two times a week to make sweaters and afghans. We then distribute our products to meaningful organizations across the nation, like Volunteers of America or veterans groups.

> —ANONYMOUS
> LOS ANGELES, CALIFORNIA
> YEARS RETIRED: 10

. . . .

RIGHT AFTER I RETIRED FROM EDUCATION, I was lobbied to run for the school board, and I've been on it ever since—for a time as the president. A lot of people asked me to run for the city council, but I felt I knew a lot more about schools than about city government. This gives me a sense of purpose: I'm doing something for young people, who are the mainstay of our community.

> —J.L.
> CENTRALIA, WASHINGTON
> YEARS RETIRED: 9

WHAT YOU DO IN RETIREMENT has to do with how you felt about the work you did. Retirement, for me, was leaving something I loved to do. And if there were opportunities to use those skills and relationships and contacts that didn't mean I was meeting a payroll and hiring and firing and dealing with boards, I would consider that a continuation of having a good time. If you did something you love to do and you can carry that work, those skills, those insights into something else for continued pay, I would say, why not?

—*SUZIE*
SAN RAFAEL, CALIFORNIA
YEARS RETIRED: 3

- - - - - - - -

THE LAST THING YOU WANT TO DO IN RETIREMENT is to sit around the house working or reading. Get up and out in the fresh air, even if it is just to take walks or ride a bike. Exercise cleanses the mind and body. I exercise at the YMCA, and play golf and platform tennis.

—*C. WILLIAM JONES*
EASTON, MARYLAND

- - - - - - - -

PLAY BOCCE: There's much more skill involved in that game than horseshoes, which many of my friends play. And it just looks better. Probably the best part is that anybody watching you play probably has no idea of the rules, so they always think you're better than you are.

—*MARK TOOMEY*
BOARDMAN, OHIO

- - - - - - - -

I ENJOY READING: I never had time to do that when I was working and raising kids. I also enjoy going fishing. I even went to Cancún, Mexico, with my daughter. You can only clean the house and do the laundry so many times.

—*C.L.*
CLIMAX SPRINGS, MISSOURI
YEARS RETIRED: 5

A DECISION MADE FOR OTHERS

I DIDN'T RETIRE; I WAS RETIRED. It's a big difference. The company I worked for went bankrupt. I was two months short of 30 years. I wasn't really ready for retirement. Whenever your wife is working, and there's just the two of you, and you're at home by yourself, you can only do so much yard work. So, I started looking for more things to do. I didn't want to work; I just wanted the things I enjoyed doing to fill my day. I started helping the Red Cross with blood drives, and then I drove people to their doctor's appointments and the hospital. And I found that it was something I really enjoyed.

Then I found an organization called SMILES. They have a therapeutic riding stable with 20 horses. They work with handicapped children. Since I was raised on a farm and had a farm of my own for many years and had worked with horses, I started working with the horses there. But it wasn't too long before they had me working with the students. I had never worked with handicapped children and was always uncomfortable around handicapped people. But they insisted that I start helping with the kids. I found out, the more I got involved, the more rewarding it became. It became a passion.

When Hurricane Katrina happened, I asked the Red Cross, "Can I go down there?" They said, "You're not trained to do that kind of assistance." So I started training and working with the Red Cross locally with their disaster assistance team and responding to people who had a fire in their houses. Since then I have been on national calls, mainly for flooding.

Then, through the Presbyterian Church, I started leading mission groups to New Orleans and Gulfport to rebuild houses. Last year, I led five groups. You go down and see the need that's still there, and it's overwhelming. I plan to continue leading groups.

—*DON BROCKMAN*
LAKE GENEVA, WISCONSIN
YEARS RETIRED: 9

A WEB OF VOLUNTEER OPPORTUNITIES

Volunteers are always in demand, and the choices are many and varied for do-gooders of all ages. The Internet provides access to volunteer resources both national and local, specific and general, and is a great place to get started looking for what *you* want to do. If you're having a hard time narrowing the field, or can't even imagine where to begin, consider some of the programs geared specifically towards seniors, where your age, experience, and free time are always valued.

AARP
www.aarp.org/giving-back/volunteering

Senior Corps
www.seniorcorps.gov

Experience Corps
www.experiencecorps.org

Civic Ventures
www.civicventures.org

Peace Corps (Older Applicants)
http://multimedia.peacecorps.gov/multimedia/50plus/index.html

Senior Service America
www.seniorserviceamerica.org

Generations United
www.gu.org

Veterans Voluntary Service
www.volunteer.va.gov

SCORE
www.score.org/volunteer.html

I ALWAYS ENJOYED GOOD FILMS, and so I joined a film club. After doing that for a year or two, I decided that I could do it better. I started a film society that shows foreign and independent films. I convinced high-powered speakers to address my group, formed a board of directors, and found a suitable venue. We are going into our ninth year, have established nonprofit status, and are getting great reviews and excellent crowds. It could be called "making your dream come true." It has certainly given me an interest that will carry me well through my retirement years.

> —BEVERLY ZEIDENBERG
> BETHESDA, MARYLAND
> YEARS RETIRED: 2

* * * * * * * *

I FELT THAT MY HUSBAND and I needed to be doing something together (he never had been a big volunteer). Our church has a luncheon program every Tuesday and Thursday, feeding the homeless and working poor of Atlanta's inner city, which seemed to fit the bill. This was just what the doctor ordered for my husband; he absolutely blossomed! Our fellow volunteers, who are predominantly African-American, welcomed us, nourished us, educated us, and befriended us. They have affected our life in ways we are only just beginning to appreciate. From this experience, we got caught up in the political scene of 2007 and 2008, registering voters on weekends, phone-banking during the week, mingling with folks who shared our passion, even opening our home to a string of young volunteers who definitely reinforced my faith in the next generation.

> —BEVERLY
> ATLANTA, GEORGIA
> YEARS RETIRED: 4

* * * * * * * *

I'M ON THE BOARDS OF THEATER ORGANIZATIONS IN TOWN. Being involved with arts organizations—the symphony, National Public Radio—gives us more outlets to meet people. That keeps you going.

> —ALLAN S. ROSS
> SAN ANTONIO, TEXAS
> YEARS RETIRED: 1

SOMETIMES I WONDER, when did I have time to work? My new job is taking my granddaughter to her figure skating lessons and competitions. On Wednesdays, I have yoga and schedule doctor appointments. I want to take a computer class and a philosophy course. And we're always having events like graduations, parties, and church activities. My life is very busy, but it is good. I can't see myself sitting at home watching TV!

—*E.M.*
EDGEWATER, NEW JERSEY
YEARS RETIRED: 3

• • • • • • • •

I GO TO RESERVE TWO DAYS a week and get $10 an hour, and that's before taxes. It isn't for the money. I must say, it's a pleasure to work with people who are enthusiastic to give back. It feels extremely gratifying to do good things for people and feel it come back to you. But two days a week are about all I want to give to it. I have no desire to work full time, none whatsoever.

—*LINDA AMSTER*
NEW YORK, NEW YORK
YEARS RETIRED: 5

• • • • • • • •

I VOLUNTEER AT A PUBLIC RADIO STATION ON-AIR, and the manager would like me to help him with marketing, fundraising, and outreach. I don't want to do that—I don't want to charge them for the work but I don't want to give it away. When I go there I want to do what I think of as amateur work—that is, for me, it's amateur work. I make a distinction between professional work and volunteer work. When I worked, I worked too hard to volunteer at all. I worked 60-plus hours a week. This is different from "pro-bono" work, which I've also done, but which is still working.

—*PAULA*
VANCOUVER, B.C., CANADA
YEARS RETIRED: 3

WORK LINKS FOR THE INCOME-MINDED

If you intend to continue working after retirement, either in the same arena or an entirely new field, knowing how and where to look for re-employment can be tricky. Luckily, the Internet Is home to a host of resources for job hunters of all ages, including career help geared specifically towards retirees. Check out the sites below for career building and job searching as well as tips, tricks, and training for seniors.

AARP
www.aarp.org/work

RetirementJobs.com
www.retirementjobs.com

Encore Careers
www.encorecareers.org

The Senior Job Bank
www.seniorjobbank.org

Workforce50.com
www.workforce50.com

Experience Works
www.experienceworks.org

Retired Brains
www.retiredbrains.com

IT'S EASIER FOR PEOPLE WITH HOBBIES TO RETIRE because hobbies give you something worthwhile to do with your time.
It doesn't matter what those hobbies are.
I quilt, I play mah-jongg, I do yard work,
I entertain, I travel, I cook, and I read. All of
these things help keep my mind active and
provide an excuse for regular social interaction.

> —*KATHY*
> *WASHINGTON, D.C.*
> *YEARS RETIRED: 1*

* * * * * * * *

WHAT IS THE PURPOSE OF GOLF? It may give you some bragging rights if you're good at it. But it's expensive and it doesn't give me any personal satisfaction. Helping others does. It makes me feel good.

> —*DON BROCKMAN*
> *LAKE GENEVA, WISCONSIN*
> *YEARS RETIRED: 9*

* * * * * * * *

SCALE YOUR ABILITIES TO YOUR AMBITIONS. I ski. I really enjoy it. But my reflexes aren't quite as good as they used to be, and my skiing is not that great at all. I recently went skiing with some friends, and I felt tight. I decided I was going to give it up. But a friend convinced me to go back with him. It was good advice. Instead of going on the black diamonds, I now go on the easier runs, and I enjoy it.

> —*MICHAEL CREEDMAN*
> *SAN FRANCISCO, CALIFORNIA*

* * * * * * * *

I BELONG TO THE NATIONAL SKI PATROL and spend about four hours a week doing work for them. I'm on the board of a local patrol at Tahoe, where we have a home, and also on a regional patrol board.

> —*J.D.*
> *BODEGA BAY, CALIFORNIA*
> *YEARS RETIRED: 5*

MODEL BEHAVIOR

I WAS A MAKE-UP ARTIST FOR 25 YEARS. I traveled the
world. I worked with the top fashion and beauty photog-
raphers. I made up everybody from Cindy Crawford to
Christie Turlington and a lot of celebrities. I had an amazing life. Right about the time I was thinking, "You know
what? I might be done," I went to live in Colorado for six
months. I lived in a teepee and cross-country skied to the
post box every day; my life was the total opposite of that
of a make-up artist in New York City.

Right before I left the city, I was approached on the street
and asked to model for a Dolce & Gabbana campaign for
a photographer who you would probably know—Steven
Meisel—and I thought it was a joke. I looked up and down
the street to see who was playing a trick on me. And they
said, no, it was the real deal. I was 49.

So, my modeling career started at this crazy age that
you would never expect. But that is because the baby
boom generation is still the wealthiest, healthiest, and
biggest buying population in America today, and the
advertisers want models that these people can relate to.
So I had silver hair and they were like. "You! We want *you*
in this picture." It catapulted me into an entirely new
career and I have been modeling on a regular basis for
the last 10 years. It's been absolutely spectacular.

—*CINDY JOSEPH*
NEW YORK, NEW YORK

PLAY BINGO. I ACTUALLY PLAYED QUITE A BIT WHILE I was
working, too, but now I have the time to travel around and
play bigger tournaments. You'd be surprised how much
money you can win. And I do win because now I'm getting
enough practice to be pretty damned good at it.

—*J.M.*
BOARDMAN, OHIO

IN MY ORIGINAL CAREER I was the Creative Director of D'Arcy MacManus & Masius, one of the top five global ad agencies. What I loved about the ad business was when we pulled off a game-changer. My current job title, which I took through ReServe, is Communications Strategist at the Office of the Brooklyn DA. I've been at the DA's for two and a half years. My main task has been to help inform the people of Brooklyn that the DA has 25 local neighborhood offices ready, willing, and able to help with a crisis or a quality-of-life issue. We have branded them "Brooklyn's Gateway to Help." It's a game-changer. For Brooklyn, it's a wonderful resource. For me, it has been very satisfying.

—DAVID
NEW YORK, NEW YORK
YEARS RETIRED: 3

QUILTING: A SLAM DUNK

I'M CRAZY ABOUT BASKETBALL, TRULY A NUT. I loved basketball back in high school, and then college was great for basketball, and now I love to watch the Timberwolves and the university teams on TV. But I've found I just hate the long commercials, so I started making baby quilts when they come on. I can now do the blanket stitch without looking, so I can do that during the games, but the rest of the work I do during the commercials. I've made at least 50 quilts during basketball games. Then I pile a bunch into a big basket and take them down to the homeless shelter, because there are always new babies who need quilts. It's very satisfying to know my quilts are out there, even though I don't see the people who've gotten them. And I love combining my two interests, basketball and quilting.

—JANET
MINNEAPOLIS, MINNESOTA
YEARS RETIRED: 10

MY WIFE HAS KEPT UP WITH PEOPLE we knew in high school. We now see them pretty regularly. I belong to the Yacht Club, the church, the English-Speaking Union, and the Sons of Confederate Veterans. I think these give me a good social outlet. At my age, if they weren't worthwhile, I wouldn't bother with them.

> —*C.B.*
> *JACKSONVILLE, FLORIDA*
> *YEARS RETIRED: 23*

* * * * * * * *

I STARTED TAKING PIANO LESSONS. We have a piano in our house, and at a certain point our kids said, "We're not taking piano lessons anymore." It was just sitting there; it was something I always wanted to try, so now I'm taking the lessons.

> —*M.R.*
> *SAN FRANCISCO, CALIFORNIA*
> *YEARS RETIRED: 1*

* * * * * * * *

THE FIRST THING I BOUGHT FOR MYSELF after my retirement was the most expensive pair of walking shoes I could find, and I got walking. The best part of being retired is to get up at the crack of dawn and just walk before most people are out of bed. There is such a peace and serenity in the world at that time of day, and most people don't have a chance to see it while they are still dealing with careers.

> —*PATTY MELANGER*
> *HARRISONBURG, VIRGINIA*
> *YEARS RETIRED: 2*

* * * * * * * *

TRY TO AVOID GETTING COMMITTED to too many things; days go by quickly. I got up today at 7 a.m., meditated, took my kid to school, and read the newspaper. Then I managed my stock portfolio, which takes about an hour a day. Before I knew it, it was almost the middle of the day. I started getting tense; the day was disappearing, and I still had things to do.

> —*M.R.*
> *SAN FRANCISCO, CALIFORNIA*
> *YEARS RETIRED: 1*

RETOOLING YOUR RÉSUMÉ

If you're looking for a new job or career after retirement, there's a good chance you haven't had to hand anyone your résumé in a while. You may be changing careers entirely, but even if you aren't, the job market has changed, and so have *you*. Rather than let these facts discourage you, capitalize on your status as an older, experienced worker to present yourself in the very best light and snag the job you deserve.

- Make a skills-based résumé, rather than a chronological one. While the depth of your experience may be impressive, a long list of jobs can be tedious to read through, and might show off your age in more clarity than you'd like. Some jobs were minor in the grand scheme of your working life, or were held too long ago to seem pertinent—but if they could be valuable for your job search today, you might want to do them credit by highlighting the skills or lessons they provided, rather than listing them. Be concise, and over all, be *relevant*.

- Consider making more than one résumé (there's no law against it!) for different sorts of jobs you might be looking for. Don't overburden a résumé aimed at nonprofits with details of your technical engineering certifications; those are best used on your engineering résumé. Again, topicality is key, and even more so when you're looking for jobs in a variety of fields.

- How can you apply your skills to a new arena? Be creative! Pick and choose those skills and experience you think best suit the area you want to move into, and be descriptive about how you'd apply them in a new field.

- It's now acceptable and even standard practice to send résumés and cover letters via e-mail. If you know how (or can find out!), send your résumés as PDFs so that your formatting will remain the same once the document is downloaded and opened on your employer's computer.

- For more tips, check out the article *Quick Résumé Fixes* at AARP.org—look under the "Job Hunting" page in the "Work" section of the website.

I VOLUNTEER IN A MULTITUDE OF LITTLE WAYS EACH DAY. Someone needs help, and I step in. I'm the one who gets the walker ready for the table mate who's ready to go, or moves a chair, or helps someone with their coat, or holds open a door, or closes a door when outside noise is making it hard to hear during a program—small but useful things that I hope go unnoticed. I also do some regular little tasks, like typing people's poetry or essays for our house literary publication; I maintain a database for the house monthly play-reading program; I've cataloged the one-act plays available in our house library so it's easy to find which book they are in; I help with props and filming, and perform in many productions; I am chair of our local League of Women Voters; I help with mailings and money-making projects; I give rides to appointments when requested. I'm very active in my church. I also have participated in many studies—osteoporosis, two long-term Alzheimer studies which include mental and physical testing, and I have volunteered my brain to the "U" for study when I die.

 —*B.D.*
  SEATTLE, WASHINGTON
  YEARS RETIRED: 18

I'M ON THE BOARDS of the English Speaking Unnion and the Chicago Symphony Ladies' Auxiliary, and I'm very involved in church activities. There are far more cultural events in the city than I can ever attend. I'm as busy as I want to be.

> —*L.F.*
> *CHICAGO, ILLINOIS*

· · · · · · · ·

NOW IT'S ALL BEGINNING to make sense to me—life in terms of serving people. A friend of mine told me his high school basketball coach said to him, "You are destined to do great things." It wasn't until he was in his 60s that he realized what that great thing was. And that's the way I feel now.

> —*TIM WILL*
> *RUTHERFORD COUNTY, NORTH CAROLINA*
> *YEARS RETIRED: NOYB*

· · · · · · · ·

MY ONLY HOBBY IS SLEEPING LATE, reading the entire newspaper, and then lying down for a midmorning nap. But other days I take it easy.

> —*JORGEN PATSILEVAS*
> *SALEM, OHIO*
> *YEARS RETIRED: 2*

· · · · · · · ·

IT'S NOT LIKE I AM SEARCHING the globe to find the perfect thing. I am taking more time to enjoy my family and contribute back to the community.

> —*MITCH COHEN*
> *MILL VALLEY, CALIFORNIA*
> *YEARS RETIRED: 2*

· · · · · · · ·

I FOUND TIME TO GET BACK to my passion: salsa dancing!

> —*DEE*
> *OAK LAWN, ILLINOIS*
> *YEARS RETIRED: 1*

NEED MORE IDEAS?

I FINALLY HAVE THE TIME to write bad novels.

> —*B.L.*
> *SAN JOSE, CALIFORNIA*
> *YEARS RETIRED: 8*

• • • • • • • •

I PLAY WII BOWLING EVERY DAY. I just competed in my second Wii Bowling tournament in the NSL Games. It's so much fun! If I meet any retirees who don't play video games, I tell them, "You are crazy."

> —*ISABELLA HUTCHINGS*
> *METHUEN, MASSACHUSETTS*
> *YEARS RETIRED: 30*

• • • • • • • •

I SWIM THREE TIMES A WEEK. I sing in a choir. I'm active in my church.

> —*E.M.W.*
> *SPRINGFIELD, MISSOURI*
> *YEARS RETIRED: 12*

• • • • • • • •

THE LIST OF THINGS I GET TO DO NOW is endless: ski, fish, golf, tend my bonsai, garden, fix things, read, hike …

> —*RICHARD*
> *SALT LAKE CITY, UTAH*
> *YEARS RETIRED: 3*

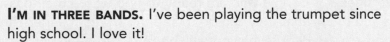

• • • • • • • •

I'M IN THREE BANDS. I've been playing the trumpet since high school. I love it!

> —*BOB RICH*
> *CHARLOTTE, NORTH CAROLINA*
> *YEARS RETIRED: 4*

MAD HOT BALLROOM

MY FAVORITE ACTIVITY IS BALLROOM DANCING. The age range of people at the ballroom is from about 50 to 92. And it's mostly single people. What's so fun about it is that every dance is an event and everybody looks so nice: People wear silks and satins and have their hair all shiny, and it's just kind of a little scene. And a woman who puts forth the effort will certainly get the attention. I'm very willing to tell a man when he looks nice. Men love to be flattered; they love attention. You'll definitely become one of their favorite people. And ballroom dancing is a wonderful way to stay in shape, because when you're dancing, you're getting great exercise; but when you're not dancing, you're constantly thinking about staying in shape so you'll look nice when you go to the dance. It's a huge motivator.

—D.S.
CHICAGO, ILLINOIS
YEARS RETIRED: 5

I DON'T LIVE ON A FIVE-YEAR PLAN MENTALITY; Bali was an accidental life change. I went over there on a vacation and came back with a big idea. Right now we are in the midst of creating programs where we will be working with major universities, for people who are ready to find where their passion is and learn what they can do to see the world change. This is post-career. People may not still be pursuing huge amounts of money, but they still have huge amounts of passion and energy to make a difference. Our programs are designed for those kinds of people. This is not just an American phenomenon; it is worldwide.

—MARCIA JAFFE
MILL VALLEY, CALIFORNIA

GET INVOLVED IN OTHER THINGS THAT YOU ENJOY!
After retiring, I got involved with my church,
my grandchildren, and traveling. It wasn't long
until I was asking myself, "When did I have
time to work?"

> —*MARGARET MCCOWN*
> *JACKSONVILLE, TEXAS*
> *YEARS RETIRED: 16*

• • • • • • • •

I STARTED VOLUNTEERING WITH KIDS, visiting nursing homes,
and assisting people with their grocery shopping and clean-
ing. I've never been happier. Helping others is absolutely my
niche. Find yours and run with it.

> —*ANONYMOUS*
> *HERSHEY, PENNSYLVANIA*
> *YEARS RETIRED: 35*

• • • • • • • •

THE YEAR BEFORE I RETIRED, I got involved in cycling. After I
retired, I had much more time to devote to it, and now I cycle
competitively with other retired seniors. It gives you a great
workout, and it's lots of fun. The best thing, other than staying in shape, is all the wonderful friends I have made by
doing It. If you can find something that keeps you active,
healthy, happy, and stimulated, go for it.

> —*R.D.*
> *KEEZLETOWN, VIRGINIA*
> *YEARS RETIRED: 2*

• • • • • • • •

GET UP IN THE MORNING AND DO NOT WATCH TV ALL DAY.
Find something that can make a contribution. I'm setting up
this Emeritus College at Emory University that focuses on
helping retired academics. There's a lot of excitement about
it for me. But it can be done any thousands of ways. You
might want to be a dispatcher for 9-1-1, or you might want to
do something artistic.

> —*EUGENE C. BIANCHI*
> *ATHENS, GEORGIA*
> *YEARS RETIRED: 5*

BACK TO SCHOOL

ONE OF THE DANGERS OF LIVING IN A retirement community is that you can come down with fuddy-duddyitis. It's essential to get out of the community and be around people of all ages. I take graduate-level classes with people my children's age and then language classes with people in their 20s. It's fascinating and intellectually challenging, not to mention interesting to hear how they talk, dress, walk. I'm going with some students to Spain this month to learn Spanish. It should be challenging since they are in their 20s and will be going 100 miles per hour, while I'll be doing 40 miles per hour!

—FRANK HAWK
LAKELAND, FLORIDA
YEARS RETIRED: 3

• • • • • • • •

I'M STUDYING BIO-ANTHROPOLOGY. It is a new field for me and I'm learning much new material. It also provides some order in my life. There is a need to get up at a specific time to get to class; to have homework ready on a schedule; to have something new to discuss with my dinner companions; to keep up to date on the new discoveries; to relate to some of the other young, smart students.

—SAM KOSTICK
SEATTLE, WASHINGTON
YEARS RETIRED: 4

• • • • • • • •

I ALWAYS WANTED TO KNOW MORE ABOUT ART HISTORY. Every time I'd be watching a show or a movie and some reference to the Mona Lisa or Monet or some other painter would come up, I'd wish I knew more about it. Now I'm taking the time to learn all I can. And I can throw away those little Post-it Notes in the back of my brain.

—MARCIA COULIS
BOARDMAN, OHIO
YEARS RETIRED: 1

So MANY COLLEGES AND UNIVERSITIES NOW OFFER accelerated degree programs that are perfect for retired people. The work is crammed into a shorter time period, but since you are not working anymore, you have plenty of time to do the work at home. I'm working on finishing my bachelor's degree in personnel management.

—*BESSIE SARVER*
BAZETTA, OHIO
YEARS RETIRED: 5

When I ACCEPTED EARLY RETIREMENT DUE TO LAYOFFS, my company offered a training/education allowance as part of the package. I told the company I was going to learn to be an aerial photographer, which meant I needed my pilot's license. So they paid for me to take flying lessons, and I got my license and did many solo flights. It fulfilled a lifelong dream of mine!

—*JACK MORRIS*
WALTHAM, MASSACHUSETTS
YEARS RETIRED: 16

I TAKE FOUR OR FIVE CLASSES A SEMESTER, but my favorite class so far is one called Psychology and Physics. It got me so excited that I'm now taking a class I'm really geeked about called Quantum Enigma. I started reading the book for the class last night.

—*FRED TEACH*
CANDLER, NORTH CAROLINA
YEARS RETIRED: 3

I HAD ALWAYS WANTED TO LEARN MORE ABOUT CARS so that I could work on my own car, so I took some auto-shop courses. It's fun because there is no pressure, and you have all day to do your homework. Now I can save a few bucks by doing minor repairs myself instead of taking the car to the shop all the time.

—*JOHN PACE*
UNITY, OHIO
YEARS RETIRED: 4

WE TAKE A LOT OF CLASSES AT THE LIFELONG learning institute at the university. You pay just once a year, and then you can take as many classes as you want. I've taken classes in literature and bookmaking, and my husband has taken classes in jazz and reading the Bible. It's been said that one of the downsides of retirement is that you stop meeting people and making new friends, and with our classes, we keep on being challenged and we keep meeting new people.

—*JEANNE*
MINNEAPOLIS, MINNESOTA
YEARS RETIRED: 7

I HOPE THAT IN THIS DAY AND AGE RETIREES don't avoid taking classes because they are worried that they are too old. That's ridiculous and archaic thinking. Nowadays there is such diversity on college campuses that all age groups are represented, especially on the weekends and at night. I've found that even when I am one of the older ones in my classes, the kids aren't snickering about me. They often come to me for help. Please don't miss an opportunity to better yourself because of fear of rejection. Those days are gone.

—*PAULA DONNEL*
PATMOS, OHIO
YEARS RETIRED: 2

THEY OFFER ADULT-EDUCATION CLASSES on the lower west side of Manhattan. I'm really enjoying it. It gets me out of the house, it keeps me alert. If you just sit in the house, you don't accomplish very much. We need tasks. We need goals. It's great to have an outside school that can act as a force and drive you. It gives your days structure.

—*ROY CLARY*
BROOKLYN, NEW YORK
YEARS RETIRED: 1

IN A LOT OF WAYS, YOU CAN STAY AS BUSY AS EVER, just with different things. After I joined the temple board, I found myself getting even more wrapped up in the local Jewish community than I expected. I'm also taking a class with our rabbi. No way would I have been able to get so involved if I were not retired.

—*FRED*
MILLER PLACE, NEW YORK
YEARS RETIRED: 2

* * * * * * * *

WHEN YOU RETIRE, CHANGE YOUR SUBJECT OF INTEREST. I feel somewhat sorry for people who cannot let go of things they have done for their entire lives. Let go and change your interest and do things you have wanted to do all your life but didn't have time or courage to do.

—*RICHARD BING, M.D.*
PASADENA, CALIFORNIA
YEARS RETIRED: 3

* * * * * * * *

HOME-IMPROVEMENT PROJECTS are a good use of time. We recently bought our home, but it was in its original 1950s condition. We've had a lot of work done, but I decided to take on the painting. I painted a whole room in a single afternoon!

—*ANONYMOUS*
EL PASO, TEXAS
YEARS RETIRED: 2

* * * * * * * *

RETIREMENT IS SOMETHING you have to wean yourself into. I taught school for so many years that I missed the children when I retired, so I tutored for a few years until I was ready to quit completely. It takes three to five years until you are ready to relax. Try new things and see what fits you and your lifestyle.

—*MARGARET MCCOWN*
JACKSONVILLE, TEXAS
YEARS RETIRED: 16

RETIREMENT TO-DOS

For years I have been talking about what I will do. I finally sat down and made a long list of things that have been floating around in my head. Some examples:

- Read a book from cover to cover without stopping for things like work and obligations (I have about 30 books waiting for me).

- Paint my house and fix the gutters.

- Organize some other gardeners and help out at the local school or with senior citizens who need help with their yards.

- Visit all the friends I have been promising to visit over the years.

- Go with a friend for a month or longer on a hiking/camping trip in Alaska.

- Start leading retiree outings with an outdoor group that I used to actively participate in.

- Do a house exchange with people from German- and French-speaking countries so that I can develop my skills in these languages.

The latest addition to the list is to volunteer at national parks. It's free. I found out about it while reading a murder mystery. The book mentioned an opportunity in the Dry Tortugas. I researched it on the Internet and found it was for real and just one of many volunteer opportunities provided by the National Park Service. I'm now excited about volunteering in a variety of parks across the nation.

—Phil Mackall
Arlington, Virginia
Years retired: 1

VOLUNTEERING AT A HOSPICE ORGANIZATION has been a challenge; the volunteer coordinator is slowly starting to give me more responsibility, but the rest of the office still treats me like a "gofer." During all my time there, no one has asked what my talents are and what I am capable of. They have only asked me to assemble packets of different forms and to laminate. Working with the Atlanta Regional Commission Area on Aging, on the other hand, is fantastic. They treat me like an adult, with adult capabilities and expectations. They provide the initial training and expect that I learn it and provide that information to others.

> —*CECELIA WRAY*
> *ATLANTA, GEORGIA*
> *YEARS RETIRED: LESS THAN 1*

• • • • • • • • •

GENEALOGY IS A GREAT ACTIVITY WHEN YOU'RE RETIRED. It had always been in the back of my mind, and I toyed with the idea when the kids were little, but I never did anything about it. But as you get older, you realize, "If I don't do this, no one else will." And it's your responsibility to find this information, to talk to the few older relatives you have left and pass it along to future generations.

> —*ANONYMOUS*
> *WOODBURY, MINNESOTA*
> *YEARS RETIRED: 9*

• • • • • • • • •

OK. WHAT'S THAT LIST OF ALL THOSE THINGS you wanted to do before you died? You want to try skydiving? You want to take up a new hobby? Do you want to go to a country you've never been to before? Do you want to learn about archeology or something you never got to study when you were younger because you were busy raising kids or something else? What's next!?! I mean, I started skydiving when I was 48.

> —*CINDY JOSEPH*
> *NEW YORK, NEW YORK*

AT SOME POINT, motorcycles and diving will be difficult to impossible to do. That's when I will have to switch to less motorcycle and more photography; less scuba diving and more oil painting (I've always wanted to learn how to paint); less drums and more keyboards. The world is a big place. There is so much to do and so little time!

—*BARRY BIANCO*
BRISTOL, WISCONSIN
YEARS RETIRED: 2

. . . .

SOME PEOPLE GET LOST IN RETIREMENT because they don't have structure. To avoid that, make sure you have a schedule.

—*L.C.*
STRATFORD, CONNECTICUT
YEARS RETIRED: 2

CHAPTER 4

Not for Sissies: Physical Health and Fitness

In my life-coaching work with adults middle-aged and better, I have witnessed the dramatic changes that developing a fitness routine—at age 40, 50, 60, or 70—can do for someone's entire life experience. For so long we have assumed that after 40 or so, our physical selves begin a slow, downward coast. This dated mindset often provides an easy excuse to avoid a fitness program, even though it is now common knowledge that exercise at any age is beneficial. Perhaps the issue was finding the time, with work, family, and other obligations pulling at us 24/7. However, after retirement those commitments change, and understanding that retirement in the 21st century gives us the time and opportunities to be the best we can be, we can begin to enjoy some of the most rewarding years of our lives.

Take Anne, for example; she chose to make a brave move at the age of 55 from the East Coast to the West Coast. Anne felt that she could age best in an environment like San Diego's, where she joined a yoga center and sailing club, developed a fitness routine with friends she met along the way, and found a part-time job marketing for an organic food business. She's never been happier or looked better!

Understanding your personal needs for exercise, nutrition and proper rest can literally reduce your biological age by years.

We have interviewed some heroes who have taken up running and become marathon champs, and we have also spoken with regular folks who have learned that your body can both mellow and get better with age, just like a good wine. The first and most important step is accepting where you are right now, and working from there, one day at a time. Welcome to the first day of the rest of your fit life!

I LOVE WATER AEROBICS. I used to go with a really funky group of old people at the Y. We had great music and a fun leader, and we were really an eclectic group.

—*JANET*
MINNEAPOLIS, MINNESOTA
YEARS RETIRED: 10

* * * * * * * *

I PLAY WII BOWLING seven days a week! I compete in Wii Bowling in the National Senior League. I have a lot of fun and it's something to look forward to.

—*SHIRLEY KELSO*
METHUEN, MASSACHUSETTS
YEARS RETIRED: 20

* * * * * * * *

AFTER I RETIRED, I became really interested in playing racquetball. I had played off and on before, but I got serious about it after I retired. I am a very competitive person by nature, and I didn't like the fact that I wasn't as good as I could have been because I didn't have the chance to work at it. Now I play every day and enter about four or five tournaments a year.

—*DAVID FELZKE*
MORGANTOWN, WEST VIRGINIA
YEARS RETIRED: 5

* * * * * * * *

DON'T DWELL ON WHAT ATHLETIC ACTIVITIES you can't do. Buy a pair of tennis shoes and put one foot in front of the other. Hey, my friend, you are now a walker. Smile and enjoy the sunshine. If it's raining, put on a rain jacket.

—*MARLENE MILLER*
TAMPA, FLORIDA

* * * * * * * *

AT MY AGE, the most important thing to eat is prunes. Prunes, prunes, and more prunes.

—*FRED MATHEIS*
DEERFIELD, OHIO
YEARS RETIRED: 10

THE COACH'S CORNER

DO YOU NEED AN ENERGY DEPLETION ALLOWANCE?

Have you ever wanted to take a nap when you were sitting at your desk in the midst of work? Or left a conversation so emotionally depleted that you felt lethargic for the rest of your day? Ever had a "senior moment"? Do you find that waking up without a sense of purpose to the day makes you want to just stay in bed a while longer? If you said yes to any of these questions, then you are perfectly normal—and you would benefit from understanding how to better manage your energy and vitality.

We often treat ourselves like an appliance with an on/off switch. We expect ourselves to be switched on in response to our needs and typically ignore the important information we know about how we work best. By tapping into what we know about ourselves, we can perform to our capacity; we enable ourselves to feel energetic and engaged. There are four areas to understand and manage when it comes to our energy.

- **Physical Energy:** This is made up of three components—physical exercise, nutrition, and rest. Like building a house, our physical selves are the foundation for how we experience our lives. Learn what you need for physical energy and create a life plan that supports those needs.

- **Emotional Energy:** Our sense of self and how we feel influences our ability to perform to our capacity. Do you actively minimize time spent with those people you find to be "energy stealers"? Do you maximize time with those who bring you joy?

Understanding what makes healthy, positive relationships, and understanding how well you communicate with others, can lead to big improvements in your emotional energy.

- **Cognitive Energy:** Our brain health is as important as our physical health. Recent research has found that challenging our brains—like physically challenging our muscles—makes us better able to focus and enhances memory. Continuing to learn and challenge yourself intellectually will keep your brain young and fit.

- **Purposeful Energy:** It is imperative to have a sense of direction to your days and your life in general. The more we feel deeply committed to something, the more energetic we feel. Take a step back and think about what's important to you. Are you pursuing those things now? What is one thing you can do today to get closer to whatever brings you joy?

—B.W.

IF YOU DON'T DO SOME TYPE of strength training, you will get weaker every year and eventually wind up in the rocking chair. "Use it or lose it."

—JIM
MORTON, ILLINOIS
YEARS RETIRED: 17

. . . .

EVERYBODY SHOULD STRETCH. I do my stretches every morning and every night. I picture myself praying to Mecca, where my legs are tucked under me and I'm bent forward on the floor. My arms are stretched over my head and my spine is in perfect alignment. It keeps me limber.

—MENDELL PETER SPARKS
SPRINGFIELD, MISSOURI
YEARS RETIRED: 15

ALPHABET SOUP FOR HEALTH

Ageworks.com is the online educational division of USC's Ethel Percy Andrus Gerontology Center. Along with information, courses, and degree programs, the site offers this simple recipe for longevity from the dean of the school.

Dr. Schneider's Formula for Longevity:

Item	Total Daily Consumption
Vitamin C (Ascorbic Acid)	250 milligrams
Vitamin D	600 International Units
Vitamin E (Alpha tocopherol)	200 milligrams or International Units
Vitamin B12	1 milligram
Calcium	1500 milligrams
Folic Acid	600 micrograms
Fiber	25 grams
Water	8 glasses

FIND AN EXERCISE YOU ENJOY, that you can do every day for 60 minutes. I'm a free diver, and I bike 200 miles in a day. I say, you can do it.—you just have to think you can. I like to think I am a role model for the younger guys who might say, "Hey, he's doing this at 63."

> —STEVEN WERLIN
> DILLON BEACH, CALIFORNIA
> YEARS RETIRED: 3

• • • • • • • •

I REALIZED I COULD TAKE THE RISK of retiring at 60 partly because, as a state employee, I could buy back into the state health insurance plan when I retired. I would not have left my job if I could not have had health insurance through the state program.

> —PAULA
> VANCOUVER, B.C., CANADA

THE WOMAN I'M IN A RELATIONSHIP with is 18 years younger than I am. I worry about becoming a burden on her, becoming some decrepit old gent. I want to stay physically, emotionally, and mentally healthy and I have a big incentive to do that. A younger woman does keep you moving.

—*WILLIAM*
NEW YORK, NEW YORK
YEARS RETIRED: 16

• • • • • • • •

I'M REALLY INTO WALKING TO STAY IN SHAPE, but many people walk too slowly to get the full benefits. To improve your health, you need to walk fast enough to elevate your heart rate. You can measure your rate of exertion with something called the talk test: If you can speak easily in full sentences while walking, you're not working hard enough; if you can barely get a word out, you're pushing too hard. Look for something in the middle. It's helpful if you are walking with someone, because you want to be able to have at least a little bit of conversation back and forth.

—*BOB PHILLIPS*
HARRISONBURG, VIRGINIA
YEARS RETIRED: 4

MAKE THE MOST OF IT

Here are some basic steps you can take to ensure a healthier and longer life:

- Eat lots of fresh fruits and vegetables, whole grains, lean meats, fish, and low-fat or no-fat dairy. Avoid sugars and saturated and trans fats.
- Talk with your physician about taking vitamins.
- Exercise for at least 30 minutes every day—walking, yard work, and playing with your grandkids count!
- Manage stress through exercise, stretching, relaxation, breathing, or medication, if necessary.
- Visit your doctor for regular checkups.
- Check your cholesterol and screen for cancers and other diseases that can be treated with early detection.

I DO NOT WANT TO HANG AROUND FOREVER. I do not worry if I'm eating right or not, if my cholesterol is high or low, if my heart is this or that, or whatever else we Americans seem to obsess over. In other words, have fun! And speaking of fun: I'm always looking for a tennis partner, someone who plays badly and doesn't mind. I love tennis but for the fun of it—no scoring. Keeping the ball in play is the key thing.

> —*JUDY CAPEL*
> *NEW YORK, NEW YORK*
> *YEARS RETIRED: 3*

- - - - - - - - -

PET SMART

Pet ownership may keep you healthier. Recent studies suggest that contact with animals can not only alleviate loneliness but lower blood pressure, and cardiac patients who own pets seem to have better survival rates than those who do not. The studies list other health benefits associated with pet ownership, including decreased stress, reduced bone loss, lowered cholesterol and triglyceride levels, and improved blood circulation. And it's clear that owning a pet can mean greater opportunities for exercise, outdoor activities, and socialization.

- - - - - - - -

WHEN I RETIRED, I FIRST SIGNED UP for a women's gym, and have kept at it to this day, although I have switched gyms a few times. The women that I've met, although casual friends, have been absolutely a bonus, over and above the obvious health benefits.

> —*BEVERLY*
> *ATLANTA, GEORGIA*
> *YEARS RETIRED: 4*

TENNIS, EVERYONE!

You get so much more of a cardio workout playing tennis. No sport where they give you a cart to drive around is doing much for you physically.

> —*Barry Fitterer*
> *Cumberland, Maryland*
> *Years retired: 3*

. . . .

One of my neighbors took up tennis after retirement and, by the age of 81, has become a pretty great tennis player. We had a coed doubles tournament where the ages of the two partners had to equal at least 100. Mostly, it was teams composed of two people in their 50s, or maybe 60s and 40s. Well, the 81-year-old found a partner who was a 25-year-old tennis coach, and they wiped everybody else off the courts!

> —*Lori*
> *Charleston, South Carolina*

. . . .

I prefer tennis to golf. I just can't get past the goofy attire that those old guys wear playing golf. And you've got all that walking up and down hills and in and out of the woods. At least if you play it the way I do.

> —*Bill Daugherty*
> *Frostburg, Maryland*
> *Years retired: 9*

Do for others, and you will forget your own ailments. That is a big thing with retired people; when you're sick and you think negative thoughts, it just drags you down. You've got to get up every day with a positive attitude.

> —*James Kolb*
> *Jacksonville, Texas*
> *Years retired: 15*

FROM THE EXPERTS

THE BIOLOGY OF GROWTH AND DECAY: THINGS THAT GO BUMP IN THE NIGHT

Biologically, there is no such thing as retirement, or even aging. There is only growth or decay, and your body looks to you to choose between them. So, this is the place where we take you backstage to look at that process—at the actual mechanisms of the new biology that has forever changed our thinking about aging. If things get mildly complicated, just remember that we are always talking about growth and decay. Come back to that simple point, and the details will fall into place.

First off, you may think your body is a "thing," like the Empire State Building or a car, but it's not. It's made of meat, sinew, fat, and many other parts that break down over time and have to be constantly renewed. The muscle cells in your thigh are completely replaced, one at a time, day and night, about every four months. Brand-new muscles, three times a year. The solid leg you've stood on securely since childhood is mostly new since last summer. Your blood cells are replaced every three months, your platelets every ten days, our bones every couple of years. Your taste buds are replaced every day.

This is not a passive process. You don't wait for a part to wear out or break. You destroy it at the end of its planned life span and replace it with a new one.

Stop for a moment, because that's a whole new concept. Biologists now believe that most cells in your body are designed to fall apart after relatively short life spans, partly to let you adapt to new circumstances and partly because older cells tend to get cancer, making immortal cells not such a great idea. The net result is that you are actively destroying large parts of your body all the time. On purpose! You're throwing out truckloads of perfectly good body to make room for new growth. You have armies of special cells whose only job is to dissolve your bones so other cells can build them up again, like pruning in autumn to make room for growth in the spring.

The trick, of course, is to grow more than you throw out, and this is where exercise comes in. It turns out that your muscles control the chemistry of growth throughout your whole body. The nerve impulses to contract a muscle also send a tiny signal to build it up, creating a moment-to-moment chemical balance between growth and decay within the muscle. Those two same signals are then sent to the rest of your body. If enough of the growth signals are sent at once, they overwhelm the signals to atrophy, and our body turns on the machinery to build up the muscles, heat, capillaries, tendons, bones, joints, coordination, and so on.

So exercise is the master signaler, the agent that sets hundreds of chemical cascades in motion each time you get on that treadmill and start to sweat. It's what sets off the cycles of strengthening and repair within the muscles and joints. It's the foundation of positive brain chemistry. And it leads directly to the younger life we are promising, with its heightened immune system; its better sleep; its weight loss, insulin regulation, and fat burning; its improved sexuality; its dramatic resistance to heart attack, stroke, hypertension, Alzheimer's disease, arthritis, osteoporosis, diabetes, high cholesterol, and depression. All that comes from exercise. But let your muscles sit idle and decay takes over again.

HARRY'S RULES

1
Exercise six days a week
for the rest of your life.

2
Do serious aerobic exercise four days a week
for the rest of your life.

3
Do serious strength training, with weights,
two days a week for the rest of your life.

4
Spend less than you make.

5
Quit eating c**p!

6
Care.

7
Connect and commit.

—Henry S. Lodge, M.D.
Excerpted from the book *Younger Next Year:*
A Guide to Living Like 50 Until You're 80 and Beyond.
Reprinted with permission of the author.

WE JOINED A TERRIFIC YMCA 15 MINUTES from our house. Over the winter months I'm in there three or four days a week, primarily in spinning classes. When the weather's nice, I like to bike outdoors. We live in an area that that is great to bike in with all the hills. I head right out from my house and easily find a 25- or 30-mile ride. And we're not far from the Blue Ridge Parkway, and that's 479 miles long, isn't it? It's a terrific place to ride.

—*FRED TEACH*
CANDLER, NORTH CAROLINA
YEARS RETIRED: 3

I EXERCISE IN A POOL THREE TIMES A WEEK. I stretch and work my muscles. It helps my joints and circulation. I also mow my lawn every three days or so to get exercise.

—*E.M.W.*
SPRINGFIELD, MISSOURI
YEARS RETIRED: 12

HEALTH: IT'S LIKE YOU CAN KICK YOURSELF in the butt for smoking too many cigarettes or drinking or doing all those things, but … just use yourself up. Taste everything, smell everything, eat everything! Think of the five senses and keep those senses going. Experience everything as perfect. We weren't given a guide book. However you did it was the right way. I mean, nobody here knows why they're here or where they're going. So just drink it up and enjoy it.

—*CINDY JOSEPH*
NEW YORK, NEW YORK

WALK, JUST WALK. I walk three miles a day. It helps the bones not hurt too much.

—*MAUREEN O'BOYLE*
NEW YORK, NEW YORK
YEARS RETIRED: 6

THE ONLY WAY TO STAY FIT AT ALL is to watch what you eat. The good thing is that I find I don't have the appetite I had when I was younger. I also seem to have lost my sweet tooth. Luckily, all my other teeth are still intact. You have to eat right so you can stick around to see your grandchildren grow up.

> —*A.P.*
> *BOARDMAN, OHIO*
> *YEARS RETIRED: 10*

GO TO A CHIROPRACTOR! He can straighten you out. I believe so many ailments that affect older people can be avoided if they were properly aligned. The spine is everything. And the older you get, the more you slump.

> —*AARON*
> *ST. PETERSBURG, FLORIDA*
> *YEARS RETIRED: 2*

IF YOU GARDEN, you can eat healthier because you can eat the stuff you grow. I didn't have time for that before I stopped working, but now I have a certified green thumb. I grow tomatoes, potatoes, cucumbers, beans, corn; you name it, I grow it. And it saves me money on food.

> —*ROBIN LALLY*
> *GREENFORD, OHIO*
> *YEARS RETIRED: 1*

FIND A PERSONAL TRAINER, even if you just go three or four times. They give you a blueprint of something you can manage at home or at a club. It's been very good for me. I'd been wanting to lose weight but I didn't know how to begin. I joined a program, and all of a sudden, something clicked. I'm eating right and losing weight.

> —*CAROL GILLEN*
> *ASHEVILLE, NORTH CAROLINA*
> *YEARS RETIRED: 9*

THE STANDARD ANSWERS to living healthily would be exercise and a correct diet. But I feel there are a few more tricks to keep you healthy: Smiling even when you are hitting bottom; laughing until you are crying; enjoying the sunshine of life; and boosting someone else's spirits when they are down in the dumps. Being inventive on how you live your life keeps the positive, healthy juices flowing.

—*MARLENE MILLER*
TAMPA, FLORIDA

THINK YOUNG

Exercise has many benefits, some of them just for the brain! Not only can exercise battle depression and anxiety, it can also directly improve cognitive function, helping to keep Alzheimer's at bay. Positive results from activities as simple as a daily walk come quickly: one study showed that the cognitive function of seniors increased by 20% after aerobic exercise; another study discovered brain activity patterns comparable to those of a 20-year-old in magnetic resonance imaging brain scans taken from seniors who'd been exercising for six months.

A NEGATIVE ABOUT AGING is the awareness of human frailty. When I get together now with friends, we laugh and joke about sounding like our parents, talking about their illnesses. When you get old, things do happen. It's not uncommon to talk about these things with your friends. You ask, "How are you?" And then you find out.

—*LINDA AMSTER*
NEW YORK, NEW YORK
YEARS RETIRED: 5

ASK THE COACH

"I know that I would feel so much better if I developed my own personal wellness plan—but it all seems so complicated! Can you tell me the most important things I can do?"

I hear this question—really a plea—all the time, and I've compiled a list of essential (but reasonable!) elements for any wellness plan.

1. **Set your intention.** It sounds funny, but developing a brief morning routine of focusing your goals for the day works wonders. Take a deep breath: It not only oxygenates your body and brain but it helps you connect more deeply with yourself. I have found that clients who set an intention every day tend to reach their goals and feel in sync with their best selves.

2. **Eat well.** As Michael Pollan says: "Eat Food. Not too much. Mostly plants." It's really that simple.

3. **Exercise.** This means about an hour of some moderate activity every day. Include cardio, strength, and flexibility, and always work with your health professional to develop a program that will challenge you but remain safe.

4. **Stay emotionally and intellectually fit.** If you are stressed, it affects your entire body's ability to function. Understand what your emotional stressors are, and determine how to decrease stress in your life. It's also been proven that "exercising" your brain by learning new things and engaging in meaningful activities can yield powerful brain health results.

5. **Relax and renew.** Busy, busy, busy, seems to be the American way, but it's wrong, wrong, wrong, if you want to age gracefully. Make sure you understand what you need to do to renew yourself: Take a walk outdoors? Go into a studio and create something? Take a nap? Getting enough sleep is imperative, but it is also important to understand what other things "renew" you as well.

—B.W.

I'VE GONE TO CURVES REGULARLY for the last three years. That has really helped me stay in shape, and I've realized that it gets me out of the house every day. Then, once I'm out, I do other errands and activities.

—*ANONYMOUS*
WOODBURY, MINNESOTA
YEARS RETIRED: 9

I WALK TO WORK. Thank God it's not a long walk, because in Chicago there are times when a long walk could be a problem. But I walk very briskly. In fact, when people see me, they usually say, "Gee, you were in a tremendous hurry. Where were you going?" It's excellent exercise.

—*ART KOFF*
CHICAGO, ILLINOIS
YEARS RETIRED: 8

LONG-DISTANCE WALKING gives me a real high. I walked in a half-marathon last June and felt so good I went for a walk later that afternoon! I prefer walking to the store, bank, movie, appointments, post office, etc., and do so whenever time permits.

—*B.D.*
SEATTLE, WASHINGTON
YEARS RETIRED: 18

UNCLE SAM'S DIET AND FITNESS GUIDELINES

Not long ago the U.S. government decided to help us stay healthy. They're devoting time, effort, and resources to conducting research and providing information on how to stay healthy and fit into our 60s, 70s, 80s, and beyond. This extensive information is freely available at the websites listed below. In brief, though, here's a summary:

Dietary Guidelines for Adults
Every five years the government updates its recommendations for a healthy American diet. The specifics may change, but in this century, at least, the broad outlines have remained the same.

- Increase your intake of fresh fruits and vegetables; whole grains; water; and unprocessed meals.

- Decrease your intake of salt; refined sugar; (foods containing) corn syrup; and saturated fats.

- Balance your caloric intake with calorie-burning exercise to maintain a healthy weight.

- Because every individual has different bodily needs and health concerns, consult your medical professional or a dietician to create a "diet for life" —a plan that will keep you healthy for a long time to come.

Physical Activity for Adults

- At least 30 minutes of moderate-intensity physical activity, above your usual activity, on most days of the week to reduce the risk of adult-onset chronic disease. A longer program, or a more intense one, will bring greater health benefits.

- 60 minutes or so of moderate- to vigorous-intensity activity on most days of the week to help manage body weight and prevent gradual, unhealthy body-weight gain.

- A minimum 60 to 90 minutes of moderate-intensity physical activity daily to sustain any weight loss.

For More Information

Dietary Guidelines for Americans
http://www.health.gov/dietaryguidelines/
http://www.health.gov/dietaryguidelines/dga2005/recommendations.htm

Access America for Seniors
http://www.usa.gov/Topics/Seniors/Health/Staying_Healthy.shtml

U.S. Department of Health and Human Services/Physical Activity Guidelines for Americans
http://www.health.gov/paguidelines/default.aspx

NIH/National Institute on Aging/Age Pages
http://www.nia.nih.gov/HealthInformation/Publications/

DO WHAT YOU CAN TO STAY IN SHAPE. If you don't feel good, you can't enjoy anything in life. Personally, I don't feel as much like being active if I haven't taken care of myself. If you join an exercise group for seniors, they never push you too hard because they are afraid of killing you. They treat you with kid gloves, and that's just fine by me.

—*WALKER EDWARDS*
CANFIELD, OHIO

* * * * * * * * *

DON'T CUT CORNERS ON EATING. Too many of my retired friends have fallen into the frozen dinner trap, or else they're loading up on lots of processed bakery goods. It's a fact: What you eat totally affects your health. My solution? I grow a big garden, and I eat a lot of vegetables. I've never felt better in my life, and the garden is fun to tend to.

—*ANONYMOUS*
LOS ANGELES, CALIFORNIA
YEARS RETIRED: 10

* * * * * * * * *

I AM TAKING YOGA CLASSES AND WORKING with a fitness trainer. I guess you could say that mind and body have become more of a focus for me, and I find that very positive.

—*ELAINE*
TORONTO, ONTARIO

* * * * * * * * *

STAY ACTIVE and stay away from doctors.

—*JOAN ALAGNA*
BROOKLYN, NEW YORK
YEARS RETIRED: 2

* * * * * * * * *

HEY, I LIKE TO EAT ICE CREAM EVERY DAY, but I don't. It's hard living a healthy life; it just takes a bit of effort. You just have to start. It's really not too late.

—*STEVEN WERLIN*
DILLON BEACH, CALIFORNIA
YEARS RETIRED: 3

GOING FOR THE GOLD

I HEARD ABOUT SENIOR OLYMPICS IN 1993, from a friend who was participating at the time. I was hesitant at first to get involved with competition at my age (then 61), but signed up for a local event. I really enjoyed it. They had ping-pong, basketball, bowling, badminton, ball throws, shuffleboard, golf, swimming and track-and-field events. I did pretty well, even though I had some sore muscles for a week. Then I started entering State Senior Olympic events. I started exercising more and lifting weights to gain strength. I still exercise every day and visualize that some of the competitors I will face are also probably exercising; that keeps me motivated. I was able to set many regional and some state records in discus.

One of the good things about Senior Olympics is that you compete against people in five-year age segments (50–54; 55–59, etc.), and men and women compete separately. Every other year, there is a National Senior Olympics event. I was able to place fourth in discus in the last national event —only about two inches short of a third-place medal. I still intend to get into the top three in the future, but know it will take exercise and practice to do it. I also volunteer to run some events for the local Senior Olympics event.

—JIM
MORTON, ILLINOIS
YEARS RETIRED: 17

GOLF FOR LIFE

I PLAY GOLF AND TENNIS. There is no comparison as to which is the better sport for retirees. Tennis kills you. It's exhausting and it's easy to get injured. Golf, on the other hand, you can play for the rest of your life.

> —GARY GALLAGHER
> WILLIAMSON, WEST VIRGINIA
> YEARS RETIRED: 1

• • • • • • • •

I LIKE GOLF BECAUSE I WANT A SPORT where I can go out with my friends and BS a little and drink a little. You can't do either of those things while you're running back and forth across a tennis court. Leave that sport to the weekend warriors who still have jobs to get back to on the weekdays.

> —GEORGE ALLEN
> FROSTBURG, MARYLAND
> YEARS RETIRED: 1

• • • • • • • •

TRY TO MAINTAIN A SENSE OF HUMOR ABOUT GOLF. Don't take it too seriously. I never wrapped a golf club around a tree. But the better I got, the more relaxed I got, and now I can really enjoy it. That's good life advice, too: Don't be too hard on yourself; have a sense of humor about things.

> —ROY CLARY
> BROOKLYN, NEW YORK
> YEARS RETIRED: 1

GOLF IS A GREAT COMBINATION of relaxation and exercise. And it gets me out of the house. I think my wife and I both like that part of it.

—*ELMER GANTZ*
POLAND, OHIO

SOMEONE ONCE TOLD ME, "Put a golf club in your hand, and you'll play it the rest of your life." You know what? They were right!

—*M.K.*
SOUTHPORT, CONNECTICUT
YEARS RETIRED: 12

STAY ACTIVE AS YOU GET OLDER; you just rust if you don't.

—*DEE EYRE*
JACKSONVILLE, TEXAS
YEARS RETIRED: 6

WHEN YOU RETIRE, especially in a retirement community, there is a temptation to become an alcoholic. You can sit out with the neighbors every evening and drink. So we have to watch that. There is also a danger of getting fat. We eat out all the time, probably 16 out of 21 meals per week. Restaurant food typically isn't healthy, so you have to keep doing exercises and making good choices about eating.

—*FRANK HAWK*
LAKELAND, FLORIDA
YEARS RETIRED: 3

I HAVE EXERCISED ALL MY LIFE; I am just not a jock. I love to be outdoors; I love to walk. I've done Pilates for 15 years. It's kept me strong.

—*SUE SIEGAL*
SAN FRANCISCO, CALIFORNIA

TAKE CARE OF YOURSELF. I see other people my age who are not able to get out of the house. I am in good health and am able to do what I want in retirement. I fish. I go hunting and off-roading.

> —*J.L.*
> *CLIMAX SPRINGS, MISSOURI*
> *YEARS RETIRED: 10*

• • • • • • • •

I GAVE MYSELF A GIFT: a set of sessions with a personal trainer. I already belonged to the gym for a long time. But that was one of the best things that I did. Over the years, the machines had evolved, and I had always wanted to work with weights. A lot of people hurt themselves when they try new machines. It was one of the best decisions ever.

> —*MILAGROS BETHARTE*
> *BRONX, NEW YORK*
> *YEARS RETIRED: 3*

• • • • • • • •

I STARTED RUNNING ABOUT 30 YEARS AGO. After I retired, I wanted to challenge myself. I ran my first marathon about eight months after I retired. Now I try to run five days a week. It's my opinion that nobody maintains fitness for rational reasons. I say that because to do it, you have to make yourself uncomfortable. You have to be motivated by something else. In my case, it's to be healthy and mentally fit. Running is what works for me.

> —*JAMES EVANS*
> *REPUBLIC, MISSOURI*
> *YEARS RETIRED: 5*

• • • • • • • •

I EXERCISE EVERY DAY to make sure that I have the health to walk around the campus and get to class under my own power. If I can't walk to class, I can't be a student at the University of Washington.

> —*SAM KOSTICK*
> *SEATTLE, WASHINGTON*
> *YEARS RETIRED: 4*

IT'S NOT TOO LATE AND YOU'RE NOT TOO OLD

The National Senior Games, also called the "Senior Olympics," is filled with athletes who *never* said "never again"—not even once. The NSGA promotes yearly regional competitions in winter and summer across the country, and a national competition every two years, in more than 20 events.

Participating athletes, who must be at least 50 years of age, compete in 5-year age brackets; there's no upper limit. Moments of triumph from recent Nationals include the record-toppling 2009 pole-vault by 75-year-old Flo Meiler; the four gold medals won by 65-year-old swimmer Daniela Barnea, who began racing at age 60; and the ten records set in 2007 by track-and-field whiz (also named GeezerJock of the Year), 60-year-old Philippa (Phil) Raschker.

So, no more excuses. Get out of that chair and go for the Gold.

For more information, visit the National Senior Games Association, http://www.nsga.com.

PAY PARTICULAR ATTENTION TO YOUR HEALTH. Don't let health issues slide. If your doctor says, "Go get a colonoscopy," get it. If you have all the time and money in the world and you're not healthy, you don't have anything.

—*CHALMERS GABLE*
MARION, TEXAS
YEARS RETIRED: 5

• • • • • • • •

ONE THING YOU NEED FOR BALANCE is physicality. Studies show you have to absolutely keep active physically; that feeds everything else. First, it feeds the body and it keeps the mind active. Second, you have to remain engaged. It goes without saying that relationships are important. If you don't have solid connectors and healthy relationships then you can't go to the next step. You can never relax because you start going backwards. I don't think there is such thing as stasis. You can't stay where you are; you have to keep moving forward.

—*PETER L. THIGPEN*
KENTFIELD, CALIFORNIA

Not for Sissies II: Creativity and Brain Fitness

Do you remember the scene from the film The Graduate in which Dustin Hoffman's character is pulled aside and given advice for his future? It went like this: "I just have one word—are you listening? Plastics. There's a great future in plastics. Think about it." Remember that line? Well, I just have one word that can change your future. Plasticity. As one of our experts explains, neuroplasticity is the ability of the brain to make new connections, learn to do new things, and to handle new circumstances. So many of us assume that our mental capacity decreases with age and that there is little to do about it aside from the occasional crossword puzzle. Not so! The brain is a dynamic, living thing that continues to grow and strengthen if we allow it.

As a coach focusing on adults' midlife- and- better, I often complete an assessment with clients about their self-reported understanding and feelings about their ability to engage and to grow intellectually and cognitively. (Focusing on brain health, by the way, also leads to a greater sense of happiness and life satisfaction.) We work on what I refer to as the four pillars of brain health: mental stimulation; nutrition; physical exercise; and stress reduction.

In this chapter, you will hear from others about their insights into the four pillars. As one of our respondents points out: "The mind is like any other music, you have to work at it daily to keep it up." The reality is that every time you challenge your brain, you sprout new connections and literally strengthen your mind. And challenging your brain doesn't have to feel like work: experts highlight the importance of creativity and its relationship to good brain health. Singing, writing, creating with clay—these are all creative outlets that can actually strengthen your mind. Read on and learn more ways that you can boost your brain.

NOTHING KEEPS YOU THINKING LIKE A GOOD CONVERSATION.
You have so much downtime when you are retired, and you
spend much less time conversing with people than when you
are in an office each day. Therefore, you tend to do less
thinking. The mind is like any other muscle; you have to work
it daily to keep it sharp. It would be very easy to lose a little
of that sharpness without even realizing it. I'm reading, playing chess, doing *The New York Times* crossword puzzle—anything I can to keep my mind active. And I talk to anybody
who will listen.

> —BOB MAGYARICS
> CALLA, OHIO
> YEARS RETIRED: 2

* * * * * * * *

A MAJOR CONCERN OF THE RETIREMENT YEARS is the fear of
Alzheimer's disease. Most of us try to exercise our brains.
I play Scrabble several times a week. I do a
500- or 1,000-piece jigsaw puzzle every
month or so. Even so, old, well-used
words drop out of the mind suddenly in
the middle of a sentence like a slippery fish.

> —ANONYMOUS
> SAVOY, ILLINOIS
> YEARS RETIRED: 17

* * * * * * * *

MIND-BODY CONNECTION

More and more research shows that the key to keeping
your mind sharp as you age is staying physically active.

* * * * * * * *

I FORGET NAMES ALL THE TIME! So I just say hi to everyone
I meet.

> —MAUREEN O'BOYLE
> NEW YORK, NEW YORK
> YEARS RETIRED: 6

THERE'S A LOT OF WONDERFUL SPIRITUAL WISDOM out there in religious and ancient traditions. I try to pull from them all. I read the Tao Te Ching, the Bhagavad Gita, and other texts. The point is to find wisdom that can both enrich one's inner life and make one more compassionate in serving the outside world.

—*EUGENE C. BIANCHI*
ATHENS, GEORGIA
YEARS RETIRED: 5

• • • • • • • •

SOCIALIZING FOR FUN AND HEALTH

Recent studies show that frequent social interaction may be key to keeping your brain limber as you grow older. It appears that having close friends and an active social life can have a positive effect on memory and cognitive function, and may be crucial to fending off dementia and Alzheimer's. One possible reason why is that remaining social opens us up to stimulating activities every day, increasing the chances of involvement in exercise, new skill building, or mental games like puzzles, all of which increase blood flow to the brain and aid in creating new synaptic connections.

• • • • • • • •

I ATTEND CLASSES AT BRADLEY UNIVERSITY in the fall and spring. Some classes involve younger people and they often act surprised that older people have a good sense of humor and know some things. On the other hand, the seniors are impressed how nice most of the young people are, even if they have tattoos and rings in the noses. I think both sides win when they interact.

—*JIM*
MORTON, ILLINOIS
YEARS RETIRED: 17

FROM THE EXPERTS

5 TIPS TO KEEP YOUR MEMORY SHARP

1. **Take Care of Your Body**
   - Get regular exercise, particularly aerobic exercise. A brisk walk every day has been shown to reduce the odds of dementia.
   - Keep your heart healthy, your weight managed, your blood sugar stable, and your blood pressure at healthy levels.

2. **Keep Learning**
   - Try new subjects and activities through classes, travel, hobbies and curiosity. This builds plasticity.

3. **Stay Involved and Connected**
   - Enjoy your time and spend it with purpose: See people, go places, do things, and start projects that bring you happiness. Socialization is tied to an improved memory.

4. **Eat Well**
   - Foods high in folates, omega-3 essential fatty acids, and antioxidants are considered good for the brain.
   - Follow the Mediterranean diet—it has been linked to improved memory.

5. **Make Time for Peace of Mind**
   - Faith, spirituality, meditation, and a peaceful, positive outlook are all factors in how your memory ages.
   - Avoid stress—it compromises memory functioning.

—Debra Raybold
Director, Memorial BrainWorks
South Bend, Indiana

FROM THE EXPERTS

THE FLEXIBLE BRAIN AND HOW IT MAKES MEMORIES

In an era of increasing incidence of Alzheimer's and dementia, a few episodes of name- forgetting or key- misplacing can make even the most unflappable of us deeply, and often secretly, concerned about how our memory will fare as we age. Here's what we now know about the brain and memory, along with tips on how to use this knowledge to your advantage.

Advances in research and technology over the last few decades have brought to light an exciting (and overwhelming) amount of information about how your memory and other elements of cognitive function work—and age. Perhaps the most revelatory news about your remarkable brain is that it is a truly dynamic system, continuing to change itself based on what it experiences. Science calls this *neuroplasticity*. This ability of your brain to make new connections, learn to do new things, and handle new circumstances with ease contradicts the widely held belief that brain potential is fixed early in life. Neuroplasticity is also considered a fundamental part of how successful we are in our youth, and how disease-resilient we remain in our later years.

Although memory is just one of the critical functions of our brain, it often receives the most attention and commands the most concern; we often define "who" we are as "what" we know and remember. In its most simplified form, memory is made up of three processes: encoding, storage, and retrieval. Encoding connects the information our brain perceives with the detail we want to remember. Storage maintains this information, and retrieval locates and uses it again on demand. Sometimes these processes occur in a highly effective way without any conscious effort on our part, particularly in the case of a strong emotional connection to the information. This explains why so many people remember exactly where they were the moment President John F. Kennedy was assassinated. The basic information of the incident is encoded with all that other information—where you were, who you were with, and what you were doing—and is then stored and retrieved along with seemingly incidental facts like the weather. Pieces of information that are less emotionally resonant require our active participation to encode. In other words, we must make information that we want to remember somehow meaningful to us. Advertisers are masters at this: If I say "plop, plop, fizz, fizz," you'll most likely remember the product advertised by that phrase, and perhaps even be able to finish the jingle!

As we get older, our brain normally begins to change. It is normal, for example, to experience a decline in very short-term memory, or working memory, as it's officially called. This is what might make us forget the name of a person to whom we were just introduced. Normal changes in working memory, along with the human tendency (particularly for overwhelmed adults) to move too fast to *really* pay attention, means that as we age we begin to miss the crucial moments of encoding and storing that would have let us retrieve a name later on.

This is the time when memory tricks come in handy. If, when we are introduced to someone we stop, look them in the eye, or think of a word that we might use to describe them, we will be more likely to remember their name. If you are introduced to a woman named Sue who you notice is a snappy dresser, you would say to yourself, "Snappy Sue." When you see her again, you'll be more likely to recall her name—especially if her outfit triggers your memory. Memory-boosting strategies like this one can be learned by adults of all ages.

The more "plastic" or adaptable your brain, the easier it will be to learn new tricks to keep your mind and memory working sharply.

Some memory problems should be discussed with your doctor. Memory issues can be caused by several factors, only one of which is Alzheimer's. For information on when it's time to see a doctor, go to http://www.qualityoflife.org/brainworks/what-is-brain-health/ and download the PDF "When is it time to see a Doctor?"

—Debra Raybold
Director, Memorial BrainWorks
South Bend, Indiana

I GO TO CHURCH REGULARLY, but not necessarily at the times when everyone else goes. Sometimes I go when the place is empty, and I just sit quietly in a pew. I'm not praying, really, but just thinking about life. It's like meditation. When I walk out, I feel refreshed and stress-free. I believe it plays a big part in keeping me mentally and physically healthy.

—AARON
ST. PETERSBURG, FLORIDA
YEARS RETIRED: 2

• • • • • • • •

I SING, AND IT'S LIKE what a good golfer will tell you: You get out on the golf course and you have to make everything else in your life disappear, except for that little white ball. Singing is the same way: you have to put all of your attention into it. It's tremendously relaxing when you drive everything from your mind except what you're doing. It's very much living in the present. And also, when performance time comes, I rapture on the good music. I've actually sung in Carnegie Hall several times.

—WILLIAM WERWAISS
NEW YORK, NEW YORK

ARE YOU SHARP?

IT IS NORMAL TO FORGET WHERE you put your keys, what you had for dinner, or items on your shopping list. Most of that kind of stuff will eventually come to you if you think about it long enough. Don't be concerned if you can't remember where you parked your car; but do be concerned when you can't remember what kind of car you drive. Don't be concerned that you recognize someone but can't remember their name. Do be concerned when you don't recognize your grandchildren. Don't be concerned that you don't remember driving past the theater or high school. Do be concerned when you can't remember where you live.

The thing that used to bother me the most, but doesn't anymore, is the slowing of the thought process. Things I used to read, understand, and remember in one pass now take two or three passes, and then I might have to read it again in a few weeks. The speed of mental processes is slower. It took me a long time to realize that as normal. I wasn't getting senile or dumb. I would eventually be able to understand it and master it if I had patience and determination. I have to work harder at "staying sharp" than I used to, but it comes with the territory. I'm as smart as I used to be, just a bit more deliberate about it.

—*BARRY BIANCO*
BRISTOL, WISCONSIN
YEARS RETIRED: 2

KEEP FRIENDS WHO ARE A VARIETY OF AGES. I have friends who are in their 40s and friends who are 10 years older than I am. With some friends, I often see they get more and more morose as their old friends die off.

—*MICHAEL CREEDMAN*
SAN FRANCISCO, CALIFORNIA

FROM THE EXPERTS

5 ACTIVITIES THAT NURTURE CREATIVITY

1. Write down or record good ideas that come to you so that you don't forget them later. Even if they're outrageous, don't pass judgment yet! It might turn out that your most outlandish idea that leads you to the "Aha!" moment that often comes from thinking outside the box.

2. Do something you have never done before, like taking a pottery class or learning to line dance. Be open and childlike in your approach—curious, liberated, and playful!

3. Look at challenging problems from a different perspective. Instead of talking it over with someone else, draw a picture of it while listening to inspiring music (preferably without words). Free-associate and work with any thought or image that enters your awareness, simply allowing your pencil to put it to paper in some fashion. Look back at your drawing, and see if you can glean any new insights into your problem.

4. If you feel blocked when working on a project or trying to come up with a new perspective, take a brain break and do something physical for a few minutes.

5. Go for a walk outside in a natural setting. Using all of your senses, focus your attention on things that you may never have noticed before. Try to make connections between the things you're seeing and feeling and your own life—look for metaphors and symbols. You may find a breakthrough or a fresh creative solution there...

**—Rosemary Cox, M.S.,
LCSW Educator,
Memorial BrainWorksSouth Bend, Indiana**

MEMORY IS A GREAT CONCERN TO ME because my mother and father both had dementia. Plus, Alzheimer's has run rampant in my mother's family. Here are my solutions:

1. Crossword puzzles. At first, I was a bit grumpy working on this skill. I have been doing daily puzzles now for about two years.
2. I eat very healthy food and also take vitamins. My husband asked why I was taking Vitamin A. I told him that I really couldn't remember, but I thought it was for my memory. How crazy is that? We still laugh about it.
3. I have a computer. I'm not the greatest at it, but I keep trying.
4. I'm on a new kick now: I'm trying to do things left-handed, like catching a ball or eating. It keeps the brain waves moving.

　　—MARLENE MILLER
　　TAMPA, FLORIDA

- - - - - - - -

AS YOUNG AS YOU FEEL

Studies show that spending time around young people helps keep the older generation energized and mentally stimulated. As a result, college towns are a growing retirement destination.

- - - - - - - -

I DON'T THINK ABOUT BRAIN HEALTH because I am doing it. I look for things that are exciting. I really get energy from people. I like working on a project. That helps my mood; it helps everything.

　　—SYLVIA BROWN
　　VALLEY VILLAGE, CALIFORNIA
　　YEARS RETIRED: LESS THAN 1

FROM THE EXPERTS

CREATIVITY BRINGS NEW GIFTS TO OLDER YEARS

You may have once heard someone say, "I don't have a creative bone in my body." Perhaps someone told you, "You can't draw." You may have internalized comments like these, and lived by them. But consider: Such statements develop from a common misunderstanding of what "creativity" is, and a prescriptive idea of how it *must* be.

Creativity is not restricted to what we think of as simply a characteristic of the great artistic geniuses of all time. Creativity encompasses more than the ability to express one's self through the performing and fine arts: It also includes the capacity to generate new ideas and conceptualize innovative solutions; to share personal stories and create meaningful legacies; to build birdhouses and learn to knit. A creative act can have beneficial effects that range from the individual to the societal. The creative product could be a single person's increased well-being or a recognized contribution to the community.

According to Dr. Gene Cohen, our ability to be creative only increases with age. We often retire with the desire to refocus our talents and satisfy that nagging urge to do something new, and we have free time and energy to explore parts of ourselves that may have been left unexpressed in earlier years. This yearning towards discovery, combined with a lifetime of experiences and accrued knowledge and wisdom, make our retirement years perfect for creative expansion. Older people can also overcome society's ageism by creating a more fulfilling and self-driven vision of their own future. Through creative expression they can refuse to conform to retirement stereotypes by living more completely and passionately, growing and taking risks, finding meaning and becoming involved in a community.

The creative process generates an enriched mental environment that promotes brain health, even in the aging brain. At birth, the brain contains approximately 100 billion cells called neurons. We naturally lose some neurons every day. And in order to retain its vitality, each neuron needs be constantly executing its job—that is, being in communication with other neurons, transmitting the electrochemical signals that allow us to breathe, move, think, create, and so much more.

An important characteristic of the brain is its plasticity. When we learn something new or engage in a new experience, no matter our age, neurons respond by growing more dendrites (connectors or branches), thus increasing the number of possible connections in the neural network. Being immersed in a creative endeavor is both challenging and vitalizing, and recent research is showing that people who participate in new, stimulating activities significantly reduce their risk for Alzheimer's disease.

Exercising our creative potential also nurtures a flexible, mature mind that is more open to new insights, thoughts, possibilities and behaviors in other areas of our lives. Today's world requires us to be able to "think outside the box." Developing our creative potential enables us to more effectively meet the complex challenges of modern living with an open and elastic mind, rather than become entrenched in old and habitual patterns of thought.

—**Rosemary Cox, M.S.,**
LCSW Educator,
Memorial BrainWorksSouth Bend, Indiana

YOUTH HAS CONFIDENCE, CURIOSITY, and enthusiasm. If you can maintain those three things in life, you can be as youthful as you want to be.

—*MICHAEL CREEDMAN*
SAN FRANCISCO, CALIFORNIA

• • • • • • • •

I'VE ENJOYED GOOD HEALTH BECAUSE I'm a natural optimist. It's also important to know that one who is not a natural optimist can learn to be optimistic. Learning to be one is important and helps people to survive and live healthier and happier and longer.

—*FRANCES LOMAS FELDMAN*
PASADENA, CALIFORNIA
YEARS RETIRED: 24

• • • • • • • •

IF YOU DON'T FIND SOMETHING to keep your mind active, it will wither and die, just like any other unused muscle in the body. I play chess every single day. And I win.

—*RALPH DINARDO*
STRUTHERS, OHIO
YEARS RETIRED: 4

• • • • • • • •

I TAKE CLASSES AT UCLA in a thing called the senior scholars program, taking classes with the students. I am sure many other colleges have a similar program. I take a class every year in something of interest to me: politics, economics, or anything that I see in the schedule. It's good brain food; it makes you think.

—*BOB WALDORF*
LOS ANGELES, CALIFORNIA
YEARS RETIRED: 11

FROM THE EXPERTS

10 BRAIN EXERCISES FOR EVERYONE

1. **Exercise your brain with mentally challenging activities,** such as word or number puzzles, spatial-relations games, computer games designed to test cognitive functioning, and deductive reasoning puzzles.
2. **Learn memory strategies.** Loads of tools and techniques exist to improve your recall; try them out.
3. **Do things that require multiple levels of coordination.** Take yoga or tai chi lessons; go bowling or swimming; play tennis; or try choreographed dance. These activities use both sides of our bodies to improve balance and flexibility, and test our short-term memory and attention span.
4. **Laugh often and play more.** It is widely agreed that unstructured play and laughter are good for your brain.
5. **Stay connected.** The sense of belonging that comes with being part of a group activity or a network of people (even over the Internet) has been found to improve overall health.
6. **Spend time outdoors in natural environments.**
7. **Get more oxygen.** Your brain is hungry for it. Staying active will help oxygenate your brain.
8. **Manage your stress.** Yoga and tai chi can benefit your mind as well as your body. Meditation and spending more time in natural settings can also reduce stress.
9. **Choose optimism and gratitude.** Those who practice gratitude daily have improved long-term health.
10. **Be curious.** Curiosity brings new learning, new thinking, and new experiences, all of which promote neuroplasticity.

—Debra Raybold
Memorial Brainworks

On the Road: Why Stay Home?

I f your mental picture of a retired traveler is limited to group tours and sunning on a cruise ship, think again. Today's retirees are adventurers, volunteers, art lovers and wisdom seekers. They are singles meeting like-minded folks on group experiences; grandparents creating lasting family memories; couples experiencing long-awaited "trips of a lifetime"; and individuals interested in self-discovery. For years you have probably had the single option of taking "vacation time"—defined as a limited period away from work. That's changed. What used to be vacation travel has morphed into experiential travel that may still be based on budget but is probably not dependent on a two-week window.

In this chapter you'll hear from folks who have gone from a lifetime largely without travel, to lengthy tours of every continent including North America. Others have taken the opportunity to combine travel with volunteering overseas. You will also hear from people who have reconnected with college friends and feel as though they haven't missed a beat. Still others add a dash of humor and adventure to their planning with a blindfold and dart. What will your travel strategy be? Read on for inspiration.

THE COAST OF MAINE, THE GLACIERS IN ALASKA, the historic buildings in Boston, the hills of San Francisco, the active volcano in Hawaii: These are all new entries in my memory bank since retiring.

—*JANE HULMAN*
BETHESDA, MARYLAND
YEARS RETIRED: 11

• • • • • • • •

MY HUSBAND POINTED OUT RECENTLY that we were free to go wherever we wanted or to live wherever we wanted. Our retirement checks are going to come no matter where we are. That's a nice feeling—not being tied to a place, a job, or a daily responsibility.

—*SUSAN*
TAYLOR, TEXAS
YEARS RETIRED: 3

• • • • • • • •

WE BIKED FROM PISA TO VENICE. Everything about it was great: the food, the hotels, the sights, the people. We didn't want it to end. And it was pretty easy, about 20 to 40 miles a day. There was one hard day when we climbed the Apennines, and it was 100 degrees and there were trucks spewing blue smoke. But then we got to the top and drank wine for two hours, and then it was downhill and shady on the other side.

—*JIMBO*
MINNEAPOLIS, MINNESOTA
YEARS RETIRED: 14

• • • • • • • •

WHEN WE TRAVEL, WE GO TO ELDERHOSTELS. We really like them, and I've always thought the housing was fine. You do have to be flexible; if you go to Costa Rica, they're going to feed you rice and beans.

—*JANET*
MINNEAPOLIS, MINNESOTA
YEARS RETIRED: 10

I'VE BEEN IN CONTACT WITH MY OLD COLLEGE FRIENDS. About 12 of us lived together on the same floor in a dorm in college, and we had a ball. I hadn't seen some of them in 20 years, and yet when we got together at the beach, we picked up right where we left off. When you're retired, you need to make plans like that with old friends. We're all getting together again this summer, and I can't wait.

—H.I.H.
DURHAM, NORTH CAROLINA
YEARS RETIRED: 7

GET A HUGE MAP OF THE UNITED STATES. Put it up on the wall. Put on a blindfold. Get a dart. Throw the dart at the map, and make your destination the place where the dart lands. It's great to plan a trip to somewhere you've never been and would otherwise never go. You can find fun and adventure anywhere you go. The first time I did it, we ended up going to Fowler, Kansas. It was a great little town that I would have never, ever seen otherwise.

—BENNY TADFORD
YOUNGSTOWN, OHIO
YEARS RETIRED: 3

I NEVER TRAVELED BEFORE; now I am on the road three or four times a year to Africa, to Haiti. To hop over to San Francisco and then to Boston is now everyday fare for me. The trajectory of my life—of our lives—not only on the grand scale but on a daily basis, has changed completely. If we didn't know it was us, we wouldn't recognize us.

—STEVE ALDERMAN
WESTCHESTER COUNTY, NEW YORK

TAKE THE TRAIN wherever possible.

—SAM KOSTICK
SEATTLE, WASHINGTON
YEARS RETIRED: 4

WHEN MY HUSBAND AND I WERE WORKING, we always felt we should spend our vacation time together. We continued to take vacations together for the first few years after we retired. Then it dawned on us: I didn't care to go off-roading in Colorado, and he didn't care to go gambling in Las Vegas. We were ruining the other one's good time. A couple of years ago, we started taking separate vacations. My husband goes to Colorado with his brother. I go to Vegas with my daughter or friends. We both come home happy. We're together all the time, so it's good to get away. We miss each other until we get back.

—*C.L.*
CLIMAX SPRINGS, MISSOURI
YEARS RETIRED: 5

• • • • • • • •

COMMERCIAL CRUISE LINES ARE NOT OUR STYLE: I'm not interested in sailing around the world in a horizontal Hyatt hotel. On a cruise ship, the average age is 63. But Semester at Sea is filled with people who are young; the average age is probably 22. The Semester at Sea is literally a trip around the world in a horizontal dormitory filled with people with raging hormones, none of which are mine. But it's a great way to see 10 different countries. If you are interested in seeing the world aboard a ship and can tolerate living 100 days with people who are much younger than you, give it a go.

—*ROBERT L. ZIMDAHL*
FORT COLLINS, COLORADO
YEARS RETIRED: 1

• • • • • • • •

RETIREMENT IS IDEAL FOR DAY TRIPS: the beach, amusement parks (without kids!), or antiquing in nearby villages.

—*T.S.*
TAMPA, FLORIDA
YEARS RETIRED: 12

I LOVE TRAVELING ON GROUP BUS TOURS run by companies like AAA. They are fun and a great way to meet people and see new places. And it's much more cost-effective than going alone. I recently went to Gatlinburg, Tennessee, and I met people on the trip who I know will be lifelong friends. To me, the biggest benefit is that I don't have to do the driving: Amen to that.

> —*ROSEANN DICOLA*
> *HARRISONBURG, VIRGINIA*
> *YEARS RETIRED: 3*

KID-FRIENDLY

National parks are great for traveling with grandchildren. Park rangers offer educational programs that help build an appreciation for history, nature, and wildlife.

ONE OF THE BEST THINGS ABOUT BEING RETIRED is the freedom to travel when I want. When my son and daughter-in-law asked me to stay at their house for a week to house-sit while they were away on vacation, there was no question; I had the freedom to do it.

> —*HELEN REICH*
> *DUBOIS, PENNSYLVANIA*
> *YEARS RETIRED: 5*

SEVERAL TIMES I JOINED A TOUR GROUP and took a chance on whether I'd like it and whether the people in the group would talk to me or not. I've always come back having made friends who remain my friends afterward.

> —*FRANCES LOMAS FELDMAN*
> *PASADENA, CALIFORNIA*
> *YEARS RETIRED: 24*

SHOULD I STAY OR SHOULD I GO?

IT WAS VERY EASY TO LEAVE THE CITY WHEN we retired and get away from all the cars and people. We looked for places on the beach in southern and northern California, and we finally settled on Bodega Bay. We still see our friends often, even though we don't live as near. We go there, or they come here.

> —J.D.
> BODEGA BAY, CALIFORNIA
> YEARS RETIRED: 5

• • • • • • • • •

IF YOU'RE GOING TO START GETTING OLD, the city is a good place to do it. Everything is here. Especially since I really haven't been driving so much now, it's so convenient. You can see a lot of things, even if you don't have a friend to do it with. You can go to a museum or do a show on your own, whenever you want. That's the life for me.

> —SONYA
> BROOKLYN, NEW YORK
> YEARS RETIRED: 10

• • • • • • • • •

WE STAYED IN OUR HOME FOR A FEW REASONS. First, it's paid for! Second, everything we need is within walking distance: the grocery store, drugstore, Kmart, fast-food chains, and restaurants. Third, we're on the bus route, so if the time comes that we can no longer drive, we can take the bus.

> —MARY BRIGHT
> ALLENTOWN, PENNSYLVANIA
> YEARS RETIRED: 10

ONE OF THE CONSIDERATIONS in relocating after retirement is, how are you going to restructure your life to be in the same environment that you have been in. When work consumes your week, that's what defines the opportunities you have for the rest of your life. Once you retire, are you going to have enough activities to fill that new void of 10 hours a day, five days a week? A lot of people didn't think of that and as a result were unhappy after retiring and ended up relocating afterward. Sometimes there are things that make it easy to stay in the same place—grandkids, hobbies, country clubs can make it easy. One of the other key factors will be how many of your close friends are going to leave. On day one, you think everything's going to stay the same. Then three years later, you find out that some of the key people in your groups have moved.

> —*FRED TEACH*
> *CANDLER, NORTH CAROLINA*
> *YEARS RETIRED: 3*

· · · · · · · · ·

WE WERE REAL NEW YORK CITY PEOPLE; we had our careers there, we raised our kids there. By 2001, both my kids left New York and both our jobs had dried up, and we kind of looked at each other one day and said, "You know, why don't we sell everything and go back to Miami, where we have family?" We hadn't lived there since the early '80s. The area had changed a lot. My husband got very involved on our condominium board, and I got involved in some projects. We tried to make it work, but we just kept looking at each other, saying, "Is this where we want to get old?" We both said, "No, this is not the quality of life we want." We started to focus on Asheville, North Carolina, which has a lot of things we were looking for, and ultimately moved there.

> —*CAROL GILLEN*
> *ASHEVILLE, NORTH CAROLINA*
> *YEARS RETIRED: 9*

SOME OF THESE NEW RETIREMENT VILLAGES are like summer camp for older folks. We visited some friends who lived in one where we were considering moving, and on any given day, there were half-a-dozen classes or activities. And not just the usual golf, tennis, and bridge. They offered yoga, painting, woodworking, stained glass, and all sorts of oddball classes. It was mind-boggling!

—*BONNIE DULFON*
WALTHAM, MASSACHUSETTS
YEARS RETIRED: 3

· · · · · · · · ·

IF YOU HAVE THE MEANS, BUY A CONDO ON A BEACH. We have one in northwestern Florida. Not a beach house; a condo. It's roomy enough for a few families to stay there, so we use it to visit and vacation with our kids and grandkids. But when we're not there, we don't have to worry about upkeep. We can have someone with the building check on it and fix any problems. With a beach house, we'd have more room, but we'd be on our own with the upkeep. That's not something you want to worry about in retirement.

—*E.R.*
TAMPA, FLORIDA
YEARS RETIRED: 10

· · · · · · · · ·

THERE IS A SENIOR HOUSING HIGH-RISE IN MY TOWN that is extremely hard to get into. They put you on a waiting list until an apartment opens up. I just got the call last year, and I absolutely love the place. The morbid part is that you know nobody is moving out of there willingly. They are only leaving when they die. I guess one person's loss is another person's gain. If there is one of these kinds of places in your town, you should check it out. It sure beats a nursing home.

HOME Sweet HOME

—*BETSY ANDERSEN*
CANFIELD, OHIO

ONE THING YOU NEED TO CONSIDER when moving somewhere to retire is how good the city's health care system is. It's more of a concern when you're older.

—*BOB RICH*
CHARLOTTE, NORTH CAROLINA
YEARS RETIRED: 5

* * * * * * * *

IF YOU'RE MOVING, WAIT TO BUY A HOUSE, even if you think you know the area. We sold our home in Ohio and decided to live in Charlotte for a year before buying a house. It's the best way to really get to know a new area. When we found ours, we loved it right away. The housing development has a sports complex, a huge pool, book clubs and gourmet food clubs, and even an empty-nesters group. We went to an empty-nesters dance last night.

—*DONNA RICH*
CHARLOTTE, NORTH CAROLINA
YEARS RETIRED: 4

* * * * * * * *

DON'T STAY IN YOUR HOMETOWN. Move about three or four hours away from your kids. That way, you can see them on holidays, birthdays, and during emergencies, but you're not constantly in their hair.

—*GARY D. GALLAGHER*
WILLIAMSON, WEST VIRGINIA
YEARS RETIRED: 1

* * * * * * * *

I HAVE 40 ACRES. IT'S QUIET. A school bus and a car went by this morning. I was in New York City a couple of weeks ago, and I thought, this is cruel and unusual punishment. Living quietly is, for me, a good thing. Other people love the tumult of the city; I'm not one of them. My wife and I intend to live here until we die, if we can.

—*ROBERT L. ZIMDAHL*
FORT COLLINS, COLORADO
YEARS RETIRED: 1

I INTEND TO REMAIN IN NEW YORK CITY. I see my future here. It just offers so much, and public transportation makes it easy to get around. I know the climate is problematic sometimes. But New York is where I choose to remain. I don't want to retire to a community that doesn't have some range of ages. My parents retired to Florida. They went to a community where they had friends who were similar ages. And it worked for a few years, and then people gradually started to get sick and die. It became in my mind a negative thing.

—*LINDA AMSTER*
NEW YORK, NEW YORK
YEARS RETIRED: 5

I DON'T WANT TO MOVE. I find it more stimulating to be in my home where I have the things I love, where I can still entertain, where I can enjoy a garden that is the product of 30 years. It's a small home on a college campus. There is a sense of being a part of the community. I have neighbors who know me, and friends I walk with. It's a great source of comfort for me.

—*SUZIE*
SAN RAFAEL, CALIFORNIA
YEARS RETIRED: 3

DURING THE TIME I SPENT WITH GENERAL MOTORS, we relocated a dozen times all over the country and three times outside the country. So the idea of relocating and starting over held no mystery to us. To a lot of people it's intimidating, but we've done it so many times, we know that you can go anywhere, do anything.

—*FRED TEACH*
CANDLER, NORTH CAROLINA
YEARS RETIRED: 3

ONE OF THE BEST TRIPS I'VE TAKEN since I retired was to Australia. I went with a friend, and we were gone for six weeks. We arranged the trip so we would connect up a couple times with a group, but we also were able to travel on our own. We really liked that combined kind of trip. It was very expensive, but if you're spending that much money to go to Australia, you want to make good on the time.

> —M.L.
> BLOOMINGTON, MINNESOTA
> YEARS RETIRED: 15

• • • • • • • •

YOU ARE NOT AS YOUNG AS YOU USED TO BE, and you have to plan your vacations accordingly. My wife and I went to Maui and hiked to the summit of a dormant volcano. Once you are up there, you can hike down into the crater. There is a sign that tells you to allow twice as much time for coming out as going in because of the thin air up there at 10,000 feet. I ignored the sign and paid the price: We had to keep stopping so I could catch my breath.

> —COLIN MCDOUGLE
> CANFIELD, OHIO
> YEARS RETIRED: 2

• • • • • • • •

I LIKED THE BOAT TRIP TO ALASKA. I think I spent most of the trip on the bow of the ship, listening to the naturalist tell about the abundant wildlife we saw and the scenery we passed by. The most meaningful trip was to England, where I got to meet some cousins I hadn't seen before. They took us to the mine my dad worked in, where he lived and where he was born. It felt really strange to be standing in the place he grew up and recalling some of the things he had talked about.

> —JIM
> MORTON, ILLINOIS
> YEARS RETIRED: 17

FROM THE EDITOR

6 TIPS FOR TRAVELING WITH GRANDCHILDREN

One of the pleasures of having flexible time in your life is sharing your footloose status with your grandchildren. But like so many things in this world, travel gets more complicated when it crosses generations. Here are some things to keep in mind so that your trip with your grandchildren will create the best memories for all concerned.

1. **Make your plan together.** The purpose of traveling together, after all, is to grow closer, so begin your trip before you set out by sharing the creation of this experience. Having your grandchildren's participation in choosing a location and activities will also mean you are more likely to have a successful trip together.

2. **Remember that you are a role model.** Your actions, from planning the trip to interacting with others and dealing with difficulties along the way, will teach your grandchildren invaluable lessons.

3. **Consider everyone's health and safety.** When planning the trip, be realistic about your physical and energy levels—and those of the grandchildren. Plan for any possible dietary restrictions you—or your grandchildren—may have. Take changes in altitude, allergens, and time-zones into account.

4. **Plan ahead for emergencies.** Don't forget to carry a signed authorization allowing you to be a health proxy for your grandchild, and bring a list of emergency contacts with you.

5. **Be flexible.** Leave room in your days for a rest, a side trip, or simply unstructured time. Understand that all of the museums your grandchild seemed to be excited about during the planning stage may not turn out to be so much fun. Keep a list of back-up activities for those times.

6. **Don't forget the camera!** Ignore family members who hate having their picture taken, or who think you wait too long to push the button, or who would rather "experience" than "document" their trip. They'll thank you, eventually.

—B.W.

DON'T GET ME STARTED! I want to go everywhere. I want to go to India, Vietnam, Egypt, Patagonia, and Alaska. I want to go by train through the National Parks. I want to go to California from Chicago by train, through the middle of the United States and the mountains. I want to do all those things.

—MILAGROS BETHARTE
BRONX, NEW YORK
YEARS RETIRED: 3

* * * * * * * *

I ORGANIZE GROUPS OF MY FRIENDS TO TAKE impromptu trips. Some of my friends would tell you that these trips are some-times *too* impromptu. But I think it's more fun if you just pick up and go. It's the kind of thing you do less of when you get older. People my age are often set in their ways and have to plan for months to take a weekend trip. I think the spontane-ity of my trips is what makes them so enjoyable. Just picking up and going on the spur of the moment takes people back and makes them feel younger again.

—JANE TABACHKA
GREEN MOUNT, VIRGINIA
YEARS RETIRED: 3

WE HAVE BEEN TRAVELING NOW FOR SIX YEARS, and we have bought nine RVs! We've been to Arkansas, and we fly-fish in the Ozark Mountains, where the people are really friendly and hospitable. We go to Missouri, Iowa, Nebraska, South Dakota, and Wyoming, and we typically spend a month in Montana. On our way back, we've gone to Idaho, Utah, California, Nevada, New Mexico, Arizona, Texas, Louisiana, Mississippi, Alabama, and North Carolina. It's wonderful to meet new people and see new places and just be together.

> —BILL CHARLES
> BRISTOL, TENNESSEE
> YEARS RETIRED: 6

· · · · · · · ·

WE WENT ON A TWO-WEEK STUDY TRIP TO NICARAGUA, sponsored by a local college, to help people understand the sort of challenges that developing countries face, like environmental problems and issues of sustainable development. It was a great trip. And now, three people are coming from one of the agricultural cooperatives where we stayed, and we'll host them. I should be practicing my Spanish!

> —KATIE
> MINNEAPOLIS, MINNESOTA
> YEARS RETIRED: 2

· · · · · · · ·

LAST YEAR I WENT TO SPAIN AND PRAGUE with different friends. The best trip I took recently was two years ago through Elderhostel (now called Road Scholar). It was a "service"-type trip. You actually go and do something worthwhile and physical—say, build a new trail in a national park. You work your fingers to the bone, meet people who also want to build a trail (or whatever else they want to do), eat simple but great food in a lodge, and fall asleep, totally exhausted, at 9 p.m. in an unheated cabin. What fun!

> —JUDY CAPEL
> NEW YORK, NEW YORK
> YEARS RETIRED: 3

OUR MOST FUN ROAD TRIPS HAVE BEEN in our Roadtrek camper van. It's not a big unit, but we have everything we need: beds, a small kitchen, and a bathroom. It's our favorite way to travel. We can camp in a rustic state forest, in a private campground with nice shower and bath facilities, or in the middle of a city, like we did in Anchorage. It's like a modern covered wagon. And what's fun about a Roadtrek is that you see a lot of other people traveling in them, and you both roll down your windows and wave like crazy, because you know how much fun the others are having.

—*ANONYMOUS*
WOODBURY, MINNESOTA
YEARS RETIRED: 9

RESOURCES FOR TRAVELING ABROAD

- The U.S. Department of State (http://travel.state.gov) has all the information you need on passports and visas, as well as travel warnings.
- Travel-vaccines.com will help you prepare yourself health-wise for overseas travel.
- AARP Passport offers travel discounts to members, as well as up-to-date advisories on weather, airline strikes, and flight delays.

IT GETS AWFUL LONELY ON THE ROAD. I missed being around my kids. They never tell you that in those travel brochures. Make sure if you are going to travel that you take someone along; even a dog will probably do.

—*CHAD MORTON*
POLAND, OHIO

FROM THE EXPERTS
PRIME-TIME TRAVELERS

If you're between the ages of 50–70, it's likely that your idea of a travel vacation is different from when you were younger. Let's face it: When you were below the age of 50, you were incredibly busy. You were working, raising a family, dealing with or planning for college, and in debt (or, at the very least, concerned about finances). You were more likely to be spending your precious vacation time visiting family spread across the country, escaping on a quick girlfriend-getaway; occasionally splurging on a spa weekend alone or with a partner; or, rarely, taking an all-inclusive, no-brainer Caribbean or Mexico vacation, kids in tow.

But now your life is changing. Just as when you were young adults, you and your friends sought out "authentic" experiences—backpacking through Europe and Asia, crewing on a merchant ship to South America, or just bumming your way to Bali—now you're ready once again to savor "experiential" or "adventure" travel, but this time in an age-appropriate way.

TIME TO START LIVING

What's different this time around? The kids are out of the house, and you're considering early retirement or part-time work options. You're ready to start living for yourselves and enjoying the fruits of your labors. You want to live and travel now, while life is good.

Your life is in the simplifying stage; you don't need more "stuff." You are taking regional cooking classes and learning Italian. You enjoy visiting the farmers markets as much to meet the farmers and small producers as to purchase fresh vegetables. Rather than just writing a check, you are volunteering in your local community. You are more active, joining walking groups and targeted health clubs, and training for fundraising rides and walks. Along the way you are meeting new, likeminded friends, and reconnecting with old friends. You are optimistic and engaged.

INVESTING IN EXPERIENCES

As we mature, traveling to China, Africa, Argentina or even Italy takes on new meaning. It is more likely that this will be your only or last trip to that destination, so you are willing to invest time and money in experiencing as much as you can while you're there.

Global connection and concern: It used to be called eco-tourism. Now, geotourism is a term recently defined by National Geographic as "tourism that sustains or enhances the geographical character of a place—its environment, culture, aesthetics, heritage, and the well being of its residents". How we go, where we go, why we go, what we do while we are there, and what we do when we return, all matter to those of us who were alive and active in the '60s.

VolunTourism: Volunteer vacations are no longer made up of teenagers sleeping on the floor of a local school at night and working during the day. Today, 50-year-olds swarm to projects around the world, including teaching English in Xian, China; conserving frescos in Italy; and counting sea turtle eggs in the Great Barrier Reef. Of course, we're not teenagers anymore; we require a higher level of comfort. We also often want a shorter program (1–2 weeks), a language-immersion program prior to the volunteer project, and a culture or nature tour of the area after the project.

Intergenerational travel: In our busy lives, the gift of greatest value often is just time spent together. But family reunions look quite a bit different from 40 years ago. Today's intergenerational family vacations often take place not at Grandma's house but at a dude ranch in Colorado, a villa in Tuscany, a ship headed for Alaska, or on safari under the Serengeti stars.

Learning: We are interested in taking our passions on the road. Why not learn to cook *in Italy*; photograph polar bears *in the Arctic*; speak Spanish *in Guatemala*; paint landscapes *in Santa Fe* ... ?

Active/Adventure: We won't give up walking, cycling, golfing, and yoga on our vacations, and we'll claim bragging rights for completing the Inca trail or cycling through Ireland.

Culture and Nature: We're old enough to have a sense of history and realize that everything in the world is changing. We want to connect with traditional cultures and the natural environment, especially those most vulnerable to extinction. It's no longer unheard-of to travel to Bhutan, Myanmar, Antarctica, and Kilimanjaro. We're ready to see Vietnam, Japan, and Germany with new eyes.

With all these new ideas about travel, and with so many options and ways to enjoy the world, it's a wonder we spend any time at home!

—Kathy Dragon
Traveler/Chief Curator
www.traveldragon.com
www.thedragonspath.com

I WENT ON A CRUISE TO California and Mexico and really didn't enjoy it that much. It was sunny and pleasant, but they let you off the ship and they give you two or three hours to shop. I'm not a shopper. I want to explore. I want to get down on the ground and find a little restaurant or café. I want to sit and watch people. I want to find a historic church or building. Cruises and me—I know better now.

—*JOAN ALAGNA*
BROOKLYN, NEW YORK
YEARS RETIRED: 2

* * * * * * * *

I SPEND MY SUMMERS ON Martha's Vineyard and volunteer when I am there.

—*MAUREEN O'BOYLE*
NEW YORK, NEW YORK
YEARS RETIRED: 6

* * * * * * * *

MAKE A LIST OF 20 PLACES YOU WANT TO SEE. Then prioritize the list. Which ones are major, which ones are intermediate, which ones are minor? Over the next five years, figure out how many major ones can you afford to do. You'll also find out that the minor ones can be as much fun. The more you research the places you want to see, the more fun it is. It makes life interesting when you can meet people and share their world. That's what traveling is—it's sharing other people's worlds.

—*DON BROCKMAN*
LAKE GENEVA, WISCONSIN
YEARS RETIRED: 9

* * * * * * * *

TRAVELING IN RETIREMENT is great because you don't have to travel during the high season. It is so different. I went to Paris in October, and there were no crowds.

MILAGROS BETHARTE
BRONX, NEW YORK
YEARS RETIRED: 3

BUY YOURSELF AN RV AND SEE THE COUNTRY. There is so much out there to see, and I'm not talking about the Grand Canyon or Mount Rushmore. There are so many interesting sights and little towns across the country that you'd never have the time to see during your working life. The best way to do it is to just start driving with no destination in mind. Just see where the road takes you.

—*DENISE LABATOS*
YOUNGSTOWN, OHIO
YEARS RETIRED: 3

CRUISE MATH

When you're budgeting for cruise travel, a good rule of thumb is to take the per-person cost of the cruise and multiply by 1.75 to get an idea of how much your cruise will really cost when you include such extras as onshore excursions, alcoholic beverages, spa services, and tips and taxes.

A TIMESHARE IS NOT ONLY A GOOD INVESTMENT; it's a good adventure. We own a couple of timeshares—in Park City, Utah, and in Palm Desert, California—which allow us to travel to those places, and we also trade them. By trading our time-shares, we've traveled to Block Island, Rhode Island; Hilton Head, South Carolina; Italy; Austria; France. We've been to 10 or 12 different places.

—*ROBERT L. ZIMDAHL*
FORT COLLINS, COLORADO
YEARS RETIRED: 1

I'VE GONE TO ALL THE PLACES I WANTED to go at least once. If I were giving advice on where to travel, I'd say, stay right here in California. There is nothing that you find in other places that you won't find here. My interest in other countries is in seeing how other people live. I've been to every country in Africa except Angola. I've been to just about every country in South America. There are all kinds of adventures and people, and they're all different in each country.

—*FRANCES LOMAS FELDMAN*
PASADENA, CALIFORNIA
YEARS RETIRED: 24

• • • • • • • •

SOME OF THE TRIPS WE TAKE ARE BASED AROUND MY HOBBY, marathon running. There are races all over the world, and when I was working it was hard to get away. But just recently we went to a big marathon in Ottawa. It's a beautiful city with culture, nightlife, and great architecture. And I never would have seen it if they didn't have this big marathon there. We got there on a Friday, I ran the race that weekend, and we stayed a couple of days extra to see the sights.

—*AARON*
ST. PETERSBURG, FLORIDA
YEARS RETIRED: 2

• • • • • • • •

I HAVE OFTEN DECIDED NOT TO GO someplace because I don't like going by myself, and I don't like to pay single supplements for everything. I look for a partner to go with me, and some of my friends don't have the wherewithal to go or they don't want to make the commitment. So I say to myself, "If you really want to do this, you're going to have find a way to do it without the single supplement." I found an organization that hooks you up with other travelers, or in some cases you don't have to pay the single supplement. You're not charged extra.

—*JOAN ALAGNA*
BROOKLYN, NEW YORK
YEARS RETIRED: 2

FIDO'S RETIRED, TOO

AVOID GETTING A NEW PET IN THE YEARS leading up to your retirement if you plan to travel a lot. And if you already have a pet, think seriously about what you will do with it while you are gone. I wanted to spend as much of my retirement traveling as I could. But what I didn't really think about was what I would do with my pet while I was gone. It's been a real problem. I don't have any relatives whom I'd be comfortable asking to keep the dog while I'm gone for long stretches. And leaving the dog at a kennel is not only expensive, but it's not really good for the dog. Each time I did that, he seemed to hold it against me.

—*W.T.*
HARRISONBURG, VIRGINIA
YEARS RETIRED: 1

WE SWAPPED OUR HOUSE WITH SOMEONE who lives in France, and we spent three weeks in Provence last September. We swapped with an apartment in New York and went to the theater. It has worked very well for us so far. You're in their house and they're in yours, so you take good care of it. Traveling this way leads to wonderful, richer experiences.

—*MICHAEL CREEDMAN*
SAN FRANCISCO, CALIFORNIA

• • • • • • • •

YOU HAVE TO DO ALASKA; WE DID. It is perfect for the retired—unhurried, full of variety, and uncommonly beautiful and peaceful. Our favorite memory is a spontaneous overnight en route to another destination, when we found a little town with great food, accommodations, and entertainment, in the middle of nowhere!

—*T.S.*
TAMPA, FLORIDA
YEARS RETIRED: 12

FOR MY 70TH BIRTHDAY, I took all the kids and grandkids, along with my wife, to a resort that was located in a convenient place for everyone. We rented a house with its own pool, played golf and tennis, went exploring, boating, had massages, did some shopping. At night, we cooked big meals and played games and watched movies. We also had a family picture taken by a professional photographer (and celebrated my birthday). In doing so, we created memories for years to come.

—ANONYMOUS
TAMPA, FLORIDA
YEARS RETIRED: 10

I HAVE A FINANCIAL RULE when traveling abroad. It's this: Don't buy presents for anyone else. In other words, just because you're in Rome, it doesn't mean you have to buy Rome trinkets or T-shirts for all your closest family members. No one uses those trinkets or T-shirts. You have to pay to have them shipped back. Plus, they're overpriced anyway. Send a postcard to your family members and that's it. I've saved thousands of dollars this way. And thousands of dollars will buy another trip somewhere!

—MARTY
CHICAGO, ILLINOIS
YEARS RETIRED. 12

PREPARE FOR IT AHEAD OF TIME. Use your vacations to try out retirement ideas. Visit communities you think you might like to live in. Meet happily retired people, find out how they put their lives together in new ways, and learn from them. I took a sabbatical in my 50s and rode my bike in New Zealand, England, and Ireland and led bike tours for Vermont Cycling. I loved the tours so much I knew that I had to do more of them in retirement. My sabbatical helped me figure out things I wanted to do and didn't want to do in retirement. It also influenced me to retire while I was young enough to do these ambitious things (60) and to save every penny so I could have enough money to do them.

—EMILY KIMBALL
RICHMOND, VIRGINIA

FIND YOURSELF A FRIEND who has an uncle with a huge ranch in Kenya. That's how I got to go there. It was a unique opportunity. My friend handpicked a group of women to travel there. It was a stimulating trip. We got to ride horses in the middle of herds of zebra, go on a safari, and stay on a private ranch. It was special trip to say the least.

—SUZIE
SAN RAFAEL, CALIFORNIA
YEARS RETIRED: 3

· · · · · · · ·

GREEN MACHINE

Life on the road has changed. New RV innovations include units that generate electricity and run gourmet kitchens, bathrooms, and entertainment centers powered by solar and wind turbines. According to the Recreational Vehicle Industry Association, up to 20% of RVers are now using solar panels for their onboard systems.

· · · · · · · ·

MY RETIREMENT COINCIDED with a normal summer vacation. I spent time as I always had—backpacking, swimming and camping, plus gardening and home improvement. In the fall, my new husband and I planned an extensive walking tour of Great Britain. We donned our backpacks, bought a one-month Brit Rail Pass, and took off for a great adventure. We stayed in B-and-Bs, walked the many ancient paths, and ate in pubs. No reservations—just taking the trails where they led us.

—B.D.
SEATTLE, WASHINGTON
YEARS RETIRED: 18

HOME IS WHERE THE HEART IS: NEW KINDS OF LIVING

Close to half of all retirees (44%) said figuring out where they would live in retirement was a top priority.

Baby boomers who liked living in communes in the '60s may find themselves back where they started—in small, cooperative group homes. This emerging type of elder housing is viewed as a more personal, more economical alternative to large, assisted-living developments. "This movement is definitely growing," says Beth Baker, author of *Old Age in a New Age: The Promise of Transformative Nursing Homes.* "I truly believe it is the wave of the future."

Senior-living communities for "active adults" and assisted-living facilities were designed to relieve the negative aspects of aging in suburbia. Even so, the vast majority of older adults don't want to move. As much as 85% of those surveyed in the 50-plus age category told AARP, the Washington-based advocacy group, that they prefer to stay in their community for as long as possible.

One new idea is "retrofitting" suburban developments into what are considered "lifelong communities." A retro-fitting plan within an existing town or suburb would create a compact, walkable community—one with condominiums or row houses as alternatives to single-family homes. Then older residents in large homes would have the option of downsizing, but remain in their community with access to restaurants, shopping, and other amenities and services on foot or by bus. It sounds like a good idea for all ages.

I HAVE BEEN LUCKY ENOUGH to have made some outstanding trips. My wife and I have gone on an Alaskan land/cruise trip, visiting Fairbanks and seeing the Athabasca Indians, the pipeline, a gold dredge, and then on to Mt. Denali by train, experiencing the Alaskan wilderness. Then, this journey took us to Seward, where the cruise part of the adventure started, to Vancouver. What a trip! What an experience!

—*WILLIAM MILLER*
TAMPA, FLORIDA
YEARS RETIRED: 6

• • • • • • • •

SEEKING THE ROAD LESS TRAVELED is not always fun or comfortable, but those are the roads I remember best.

—*B.D.*
SEATTLE, WASHINGTON
YEARS RETIRED: 18

• • • • • • • •

JUST GIVE ME MY CAR, the open road, and a sunny day, and I'm a happy camper. When I'm driving and it's warm out, I'll have the music on and the windows open—to hell with the air conditioning—and sometimes I'll pass my exit because I'm so overwhelmed with the music and the motion of the car. I listen to the Beatles, the Bee Gees, Simon and Garfunkel, the Platters. I like country. I like opera. I don't like rap, and I don't like hard rock. I like the original kind of rock 'n' roll, from the '50s and '60s and '70s.

—*JOAN ALAGNA*
BROOKLYN, NEW YORK
YEARS RETIRED: 2

Making the Money Work: Finance

O ne of the most important things you will learn in this chapter is that information is power. The earlier you understand your current cost of living, the better you can figure out what income you will need to rely on in retirement—and for how many years. People are often surprised when they learn that for today's 65-year-old couple, one member is likely to live to be 92 years old. Have you anticipated that in your income stream planning?

As a life coach, I often help people untangle their wants and needs: the yearning to retire from a full-time career versus the need to continue bringing in some income. Interestingly, what we have learned is that work has often come to mean something quite different at this juncture. Even when they realize that income generation is still necessary, many people determine that they want to change the way they work in two very clear ways. First, they want to decrease the amount of time spent at work-for-pay so that is just one part of their retinue of activities. Second, even if the money generated is not as robust as other opportunities, many "pro-tirees" choose work that they enjoy.

In earlier years, many of us have chosen pay over passion. At this stage, a sense of meaning and purpose is more important to us.

Financial planning and planning for your long-term health needs go hand in hand. Challenging topics including Living Wills, Health Care Power of Attorney, and other important documents that we all should have. You'll find them described on page 172.

Of course, there's plenty of advice and anecdotes from individuals as well as experts, capturing the essence of what you need to know when planning for your financial future. Financial planning is critically important to enable you to design your "pro-tirement" years in the most meaningful and practical way.

THE FIRST THING YOU SHOULD DO WHEN you're considering retiring is to go over your finances with a financial adviser or accountant. Make sure that you will have enough income to live the lifestyle you want before you make a move.

—JOHN R. BRIGHT
ALLENTOWN, PENNSYLVANIA
YEARS RETIRED: 10

• • • • • • • • •

JOIN AARP AS SOON AS POSSIBLE. There are so many discounts that are available to you as a member. For instance, I just bought my son a Home Depot gift card for his birthday last week. When I presented my AARP card, they gave me a 5 percent discount, so I was able to get more money on the card than I probably would have spent otherwise. AARP is an organization that really understands the needs of its members, and they tailor the program to meet those needs.

—MARY CLAYTON
GREEN MOUNT, VIRGINIA
YEARS RETIRED: 7

• • • • • • • •

YOU ARE ALLOWED TO USE THE MONEY you're saving in an IRA to pay for certain expenses that your kids might be running up. But if the grandkids need money, they should talk to their parents.

—PEGGY WEHR
WOODWORTH, OHIO
YEARS RETIRED: 7

STATES THAT TAX SOCIAL SECURITY BENEFITS

Colorado	New Mexico
Connecticut	North Dakota
Iowa	Rhode Island
Kansas	Utah
Minnesota	Vermont
Missouri	West Virginia
Montana	Wisconsin
Nebraska	

THE IRS WILL ALLOW YOU TO GIFT $10,000 a year, maybe more, to one person. I'm fortunate enough to have the money to do that for my three grandchildren. I give to them at Christmas, and as you can imagine, they look forward to it. One caveat: They have to put 25 percent into savings. The rest, they can do what they want. I find that most of the time they put it in investments or buy things for their home.

> —E.R.
> TAMPA, FLORIDA
> YEARS RETIRED: 10

• • • • • • • •

RULE NUMBER ONE: Never, ever invest with a friend or family member; hire a financial planner. If I could do it again, I would accumulate a half a million dollars, open a Schwab account, and get an account manager. I would never again do it by myself.

> —JULE
> SAN RAFAEL, CALIFORNIA

• • • • • • • •

KNOW AS MUCH AS POSSIBLE ABOUT YOUR ASSETS. My wife and I do everything ourselves. There are three benefits to doing this: First, you don't have to worry about anybody cheating you. Second, it keeps your brain alert. Third, it's cheaper!

> —ANONYMOUS
> CORVALLIS, OREGON
> YEARS RETIRED: 11

• • • • • • • •

BEFORE RETIRING, make certain you understand the difference between a "want" and a "need." When I first retired, I spent about $60,000 in one year on a bunch of frivolous crap I didn't need, including boat equipment and a new car. The combination of extra free time and an "I've worked so hard all these years; why should I deny myself now?" attitude can be very damaging to your bank account.

> —JEFFREY WACO
> NEW YORK, NEW YORK
> YEARS RETIRED: 2

PLANTING A SEED

I ASKED MY PARENTS while they were still alive to sign a document that would skip my interests in their estate and let the money go directly to my children. It's called a generation-skipping trust. It's a tax-planning and an estate-planning device. I wanted to give my children the benefit of the money in their lifetime, and I would get the joy of seeing them have that extra boost to use in their young life rather than in their older life. This is legacy planning as well. I have left two significant legacies: Gymboree will live on and so will the yoga studio that is now YogaWorks. And I wanted to make some substantial contribution to my family legacy. I know people with a lot more money than I have who would never consider that kind of trust, but it seems smart, prudent and generous. I wanted to pass along that kind of thinking and that kind of perspective and character to my kids. When my daughter bought her family home using what she lovingly referred to as "Nana's money," she stood out in front of that house at age 32 and called me to say that she hoped she would be able to give to her grandchildren the ability to buy their first home. That's the message when actions speak louder than words: No money could have bought a better conversation. What I did for her seeded a whole philosophy of family legacy giving. Pretty cool, huh?

—*JOAN BARNES*
SAN FRANCISCO, CALIFORNIA

MONEY SHOULD BE SPENT ON THINGS YOU WANT TO DO. If you play golf and do it passionately, spend your money there. Every human being has a chance to do something that makes him happy.

—*RICHARD BING, M.D.*
PASADENA, CALIFORNIA
YEARS RETIRED: 3

I LIKE TO SPEND MY MONEY ON CHARITABLE THINGS. I like going to plays and the theater. I've been a season-ticket subscriber to the USC football team and basketball team for 75 years. I signed up when I was a freshman, and I continue to go to the games.

—*FRANCES LOMAS FELDMAN*
PASADENA, CALIFORNIA
YEARS RETIRED: 24

. . . .

THE MOST IMPORTANT THING I DID BEFORE RETIREMENT was pay off my condominium. I have no mortgage payment, which means that my housing costs are only the condo fee plus property taxes. I also was frugal, tracking my expenditures and cutting back in many creative ways. This enabled me to retire with sufficient savings to travel and have adventures. I know how to live solely on my pension. I am spending my first year trying to figure out what I can do when I grow up!

—*DALE SUSAN BROWN*
WASHINGTON, D.C.
YEARS RETIRED: LESS THAN 1

. . . .

TO DEAL WITH YOUR HMO, get a doctor who is really good at writing letters. My husband's oncologist saved us over $8,000 on medications this way.

—*DONA*
NEW YORK, NEW YORK

. . . .

MOST OF US SHOULD HAVE paid more attention to the financial investing we did over the past years. However, it is never too late to learn new tips. Get professional advice before moving any retirement monies to avoid penalties. "Rollover" means just that. Never close a retirement account one day to open a new account at a different bank the next day. That one day will cost you plenty!

—*MAUREEN O'BOYLE*
NEW YORK, NEW YORK
YEARS RETIRED: 6

DON'T DO IT OUR WAY!

When it comes to financial planning and money management, baby boomers frequently feel they have not set a good example for their children. Many boomers, who grew up during a time of relative economic prosperity, have not led their lives with the frugality and financial prudence that characterized their parents' generation, nor have they instilled these values in their children. As a result, many boomer parents think their children do not have the necessary levels of financial skill and discipline and are all too willing to spend recklessly on the newest car or electronic gadget.

What most people are asking for from retirement planning services is advice to help children become more financially savvy. This is an even bigger issue for those with financially dependent children—61% rate it as their top financial advice need.

This finding may be reflective of the recent growth in households with children over the age of 18 living at home.

THERE ARE ALL KINDS OF WRITERS and advisors who seem to be objective and mean to give you good advice, but all of those people are part of an industry that is trying to profit by taking your money away from you. Investment advisors are required to give you the conventional wisdom, which is that stock markets outperform the other instruments. None of them are going to warn you about serious problems. You have to read and think about it and invest for yourself. In this current economic climate you shouldn't be investing in the stock market because it's a game for insiders. And you're probably not savvy enough to be an insider.

—*PETER*
MINNEAPOLIS, MINNESOTA

THE COACH'S CORNER

FINANCIAL ORGANIZING THAT WORKS

Even if you've crunched all the numbers, you haven't necessarily organized your finances in a manner that will best serve your needs. Follow these steps to have even more financial peace of mind.

1. **Streamline your income and expenses.** Have your Social Security, pension and other income payments automatically deposited into your investment or bank account each month. At the same time, sign up for your bank to automatically pay some of your fixed and ongoing expenses, like your mortgage and supplemental insurance fees.

2. **Organize and protect your account information** and share that information with someone you trust. See those piles on your desk? Create clearly marked files and update them once a month with new statements. Keep a list that lays out and clearly describes all of your accounts.

3. **Simplify by reducing the amount of paper** you hold on to. That pile on your desk probably contains a stack of unnecessary receipts, copies of bills, and cancelled checks. But don't forget: records of expenses that are needed for tax purposes should be kept for seven years.

4. **Create an estate plan** that covers financial concerns as well as health-related issues. Decide who will have access to your accounts in order to pay bills should you become unable to do so.

—B.W.

YOU CAN'T LIVE ON SOCIAL SECURITY. It's like $16,000 a year, and you really can't enjoy yourself, or even do a lot of things you're used to, for $16,000. Late in my working life, I had tried to make different investments in stocks and bonds. In the end, it turned out to be a good thing.

—*SONYA*
BROOKLYN, NEW YORK
YEARS RETIRED: 10

MY WIFE ENDED UP BEING HOSPITALIZED for several months, and I didn't know where I was going to get the money to pay the bills. I found out that you can take money out of your IRA early to pay for some of that stuff without penalty. It saved me a lot of hand-wringing trying to figure out where I was going to get the money.

—*DENNIS RUSSO*
WOODWORTH, OHIO
YEARS RETIRED: 4

MY WIFE WOULD SAY MY FAVORITE WAY to spend money is to not spend it. That said, a good way to spend money is to spend it on someone else. I give a lot of money annually to local organizations like the food bank in my county. That's much more appealing to me than buying clothing. And I spend my money on my children. I'm inclined to give them books; I don't know whether they read them or not. And this past Christmas, I gave them each a goat! They didn't actually receive the goat; there's a program called Heifer International whereby you can give money to buy a goat for people in a developing country. I bought goats in my children's names. The children liked that.

—*ROBERT L. ZIMDAHL*
FORT COLLINS, COLORADO
YEARS RETIRED: 1

FROM THE EXPERTS

LONGEVITY VS. INFLATION: PLEASE PAY ATTENTION

Here you are: You've worked 25, 30, 40, or more years and are ready to reap the rewards of your long journey. During that journey, you've purchased homes; raised children and paid for their education; attempted to stay ahead of your bills; and, throughout it all, hopefully, you've saved for retirement. Yet the fact is that over 50% of 50-year-olds haven't saved a dime towards the years when they won't have a paycheck coming in. And this is the situation in which we find most people—on the brink of retirement, not having saved enough, and not having a clue about what they need to maintain the same quality of life they had while they were working, not to mention how much money they'll need to last their entire lifetimes.

There are two factors that today's retirees must consider. The first is longevity: Actuaries estimate that for a couple who are 65 years old, one of the individuals will live to the age of 92. For the first time in history, the older you are, the longer you are expected to live. When Social Security was signed into law in 1935, people were expected to tap into it for a maximum of five years. Compare that with today, when we see people enjoying 20, 25, and even 30 years of retirement and it's no surprise that our Social Security system is stretched to the limits and expected to be "depleted in 2037" when it will only be able to pay 75 cents on the dollar. Health conditions that used to lead to death are now being treated successfully.

The second factor to take into account is inflation. How does inflation affect how much we need for retirement? Since 1926, the average inflation rate has been about 3% per year. So, during your retirement years, your buying power will decrease by half. Assume you need $80,000 per year at age 65 for retirement. Your buying power decreases annually until age 89, when $80,000 buys only $40,000 worth of goods. At age 89, you'll need $160,000 to buy the same goods that you purchased at age 65 for $80,000. Does that get your attention? Most people plan for the amount of money they need when they first retire but not for what they'll need 10, 20, or 30 years down the line. Remember: inflation does not stop when you retire.

—**Craig Trojahn**
National Life and Financial Services Trainer
Farmers Insurance Group
Los Ranchos, New Mexico

IF YOU ARE ABOUT TO RETIRE, PLAN AHEAD. Plan ahead. Plan ahead. Pay off all monthly recurring bills. Have a complete physical, visual, and dental exam before you lose your standard health insurance. (That also includes minor outpatient gastrointestinal screening tests that should be done at about the age of retirement.) Insurance plans cost a lot more after retirement and often do not cover a yearly physical exam. Select and utilize the skills of a financial adviser who is knowledgeable in your area. Consider refinancing your house; I found a far lower interest rate. Think about making or updating your will. Consider investing in a long-term care policy and update your life insurance policy.

—L.H.
SAN ANTONIO, TEXAS
YEARS RETIRED: 1

RETIREMENT GETS MORE EXPENSIVE EVERY YEAR. I get a pension from Caterpillar and Social Security. I used to bank the Social Security check every month. Now I am spending it for monthly expenses, too. We used to travel overseas once or twice a year and now we just travel in the U.S. We've cut back on some charitable giving or other causes. We rarely eat at expensive restaurants anymore. But, we still regularly eat out, travel several times each year, and go to stage shows and musicals. We don't spend much money on clothes anymore or new cars. We are still doing about what we want to do and can cut costs more when we will have to.

—JIM
MORTON, ILLINOIS
YEARS RETIRED: 17

* * * * * * * *

PLAN AHEAD SO YOU CAN BE FLEXIBLE. My wife and I both found out within a week of each other that our companies were downsizing, and we were both eligible for a buyout package. It wasn't something that we'd expected or planned on. I know in my case, I thought I'd probably be working another couple of years. I was surprised to hear about it, but when I heard the buyout details, I became pleasantly surprised. We had to go back and think about it, figuring out whether it would work financially, but since we both had a buyout, which partially made up for the loss of income, it made the decision a lot easier.

—ANONYMOUS
WOODBURY, MINNESOTA
YEARS RETIRED: 9

* * * * * * * *

THE LONGER I LIVE, THE LESS I SAVE MONEY, and the more of my saved money I spend on my family. You know what they say: You can't take it with you. I think you should spend the money on your family while you can, instead of willing it to them once you're gone. This way you can share in the fun.

—AGNES DAVIDSON
WILLIAMSTOWN, KENTUCKY
YEARS RETIRED: 1

HARD WORK STILL PAYS OFF

I WORKED FOR 28 YEARS IN A LOW-PAYING private school job. I have always been frugal, but when at age 45 I was divorced, with no bank account, no house, no car, and few monetary assets, I took stock of the situation and saw that I only had 20 more years to save for possibly 50 years. Scary! At that time, I moved into a house-sharing situation where I just paid one-sixth of rent and utilities, shopped at thrift stores, and clipped coupons. I started dumping one-third of my paycheck into savings and my retirement account. I saved enough in five years to buy an FHA "repo" house in the central area of Seattle, where I happily lived as the only "white" person on the block (and close enough to walk to work). With much elbow grease and hard labor, I upgraded my home and yard so that in 10 years, I was able to sell it for a profit and move to a condo, until I remarried. Profit from my condo was added to my new husband's house sale, and we bought a house in a nice neighborhood. We lived there until moving into our retirement apartment. The monthly payments are largely covered from our joint account with our financial adviser, who has invested it well. She sends us a check each month, which covers a major part of our rent, utilities, dinners, entertainment, etc. That account is decreasing, but barring a major meltdown, it will support us for enough years.

—*B.D.*
SEATTLE, WASHINGTON
YEARS RETIRED: 18

NEVER GO INTO RETIREMENT WITH DEBT. I made sure I had everything, including my mortgage, paid off before I retired. This cut the amount of money I needed to live off by at least half.

—*ANONYMOUS*
LOS ANGELES, CALIFORNIA
YEARS RETIRED: 10

FROM THE EXPERTS

HEALTH CONCERNS: MAKE YOUR WISHES KNOWN

You don't want to think about it, but you must: Who should have the power to "pull the plug" if and when the time comes that those decisions need to be made. Critical documents you'll want to consider and be clear about are these:

- A Living Will allows you to express your wishes concerning life-sustaining procedures.
- A Health Care Power of Attorney designates an individual who has the authority to make health care decisions on your behalf if you are unconscious, mentally incompetent, or unable to make decisions.
- A General Power of Attorney is very broad and allows an agent to handle all your affairs when you are unable to do so. This may include when you're traveling out of the state or country or when you are physically or mentally incapable of handling your affairs.
- A Special Power of Attorney is the vehicle to consider if you are interested in giving only specific powers to the person or organization.

Nursing home expenses can average from $35,000–$50,000 per year. These costs fall under the category known as long-term care coverage. Many people believe that Medicare will pick up these costs, but they are wrong. Medicare pays only for medically necessary, skilled nursing-facility or home-health care; even then, you must meet certain conditions. Most long-term care assists people with support services such as activities of daily living like dressing, bathing, and using the bathroom. Medicare doesn't pay for this type of care, called "custodial care." Most of the expense is borne by the individual and his or her family. Similarly, Medicaid does not cover the difference. Most people are surprised to know how far your assets must be depleted for Medicaid to kick in.

To provide for this shortfall and gap, consider long-term care insurance coverage. When your children realize how much long-term-care could cost, they will jump at the chance to help pay the premiums.

—Craig Trojahn
National Life and Financial Services Trainer
Farmers Insurance Group
Los Ranchos, New Mexico

GET YOUR COST-OF-LIVING ESTIMATES and then double them. We thought we'd worked out everything about the cost of retirement. We went through all of our bills for 10 years, we got a new roof and a new car, our house was paid for. But everything goes up over time, and your income doesn't.

—*ANONYMOUS*
PETALUMA, CALIFORNIA
YEARS RETIRED: 13

• • • • • • • •

WE HAVE A RULE THAT ANY MONEY we make after retirement is our own to spend as we like. Neither of us is accountable to the other. Our income from Social Security, investments, and pensions is joint money, and we decide together how to spend it.

—*JOSEPH EMIL VUCINOVICH*
REDMOND, WASHINGTON
YEARS RETIRED: 7

ONLINE RETIREMENT CALCULATORS

The Web has made it much easier to figure out in different ways how much money you have, will need, or must save, for retirement. Try more than one of the calculators from this list of the best and compare your results.

Pension Plan Retirement Options Calculator
Lets you "sample various distribution choices so you can select the one that's right for you." Includes helpful definitions for terminology used in the calculator.
http://www.aarp.org/work/retirement-planning/pension_plan_calculator/

Contribution Effects on Your Paycheck Calculator
Here you'll "see how additions to your employee savings plan will affect the paycheck you take home."
http://www.aarp.org/work/retirement-planning/contributions_paycheck_calculator/

Retirement Nest Egg Calculator
Determines just how much money you'll need to retire securely. See your current plan shortfall next to your projected need, and find out how much you'll have to save per month to meet that goal.
http://www.aarp.org/work/retirement-planning/retirement_nest_egg_calculator/

Social Security Online's Benefit Calculators
Calculators ranging from a rough estimator to a detailed analyzer (which you must download and install) to determine your potential Social Security benefit amounts, with both retirement and disability and survivor rates.
http://www.ssa.gov/planners/benefitcalculators.htm

Retirement Income Estimator
Interactive and PDF worksheets to help you know how much to save for retirement; includes a Federal Employee version as well as a Spanish-language version.
http://www.choosetosave.org/ballpark/

Medicare Coverage Gap
For those with Medicare Part D: Check your medications against a chart to see if you're at risk for the "doughnut hole" coverage gap, and research alternative drugs.
http://doughnuthole.aarp.org/

Reverse Mortgage Calculator:
Here's a specialty item: A calculator that "provides approximate estimates for two federally-insured reverse mortgages."
http://rmc.ibisreverse.com/rmc_pages/rmc_aarp/aarp_ind-ex.aspx

WE NEVER HAD A LOT OF MONEY and we didn't come from a lot of money. We had saved money, and we thought about taking six months off. But we had a fortunate opportunity to work with my daughter after selling our other business; her business was getting bigger and bigger. Then, two years ago, we lost everything to Madoff; it collapsed us. Now working for my daughter was no longer a hobby—our business literally became a mom-and-pop. It's all been an adjustment. We said to ourselves, "Why didn't we take those trips?" At the same time I feel so lucky. OK, we don't have the savings anymore because of the Madoff thing. But the loss changes your perspective on what's important: love, family, and good health. It could have been a disaster, but it gave us great focus and a renewed spirit. We had to look at our attitude and change our paradigm.

  —ADRIAN
   LOS ANGELES, CALIFORNIA
   YEARS RETIRED: 3

WHEN WE STARTED TO PLAN FOR RETIREMENT, my husband and I sat down with a financial planner to see what our situation looked like. It's a good idea to have an expert look at your assets and financial situation objectively. Another good idea is to update your wills and create directives. No one wants to do these things, but they are important. It eases the burden, and you can then focus on just enjoying yourselves.

—LOUISE WARNER
NEW PHILADELPHIA, OHIO
YEARS RETIRED: 5

ABOUT SIX MONTHS BEFORE I RETIRED, I knew I was going to be in the market soon for a new car. I decided to buy it while I was still working instead of waiting until I was officially retired. It's much easier to get financing for a major purchase like a car while you can still list an employer on the application. It always looks good to have a job when you are trying to borrow money.

—SHANNON LIETWILER
KEEZLETOWN, VIRGINIA
YEARS RETIRED: 1

I NEED MORE MONEY TO LIVE ON NOW than I did when I was working. It has forced me to budget differently than I would have imagined. For instance, I have much more free time to shop, so I tend to buy more items impulsively, like shoes, than I would have while I was working, for the simple reason that I didn't have so much time to shop. Also, I spend more time in my apartment, so I tend to eat more snack food. It's not that I'm hungry, just that I'm home more so I eat more. To counter that spending, I eat out less than I did when I was working because I don't have co-workers to go out to lunch with. And now I don't have to buy clothes for work.

—BETTY SMITH
PITTSBURGH, PENNSYLVANIA
YEARS RETIRED: 5

IT'S NEVER TOO LATE

MY COMPANY SET A POLICY OF OFFICIALLY PREPARING
retirees five years before retirement. The special retirement seminar was not offered before that. Partially
because of that, I assumed that five years was enough
time. It was not! I was lucky; I will still be OK because, late
in the game, I met with a financial planner. The planner
helped me to analyze my real situation and to develop a
workable plan. My first meeting was about a year before
retirement. The biggest change I had to make was revis-
ing the way I viewed a mortgage. I had hoped to pay off
my house shortly after I retired, but I could not afford the
rate with the retirement payments I would be
receiving. They helped me see that changing to a 30-year mortgage and not worrying about paying it off was the best option
for me because of the current financial and
personal picture. When I refinanced, I also
included some mad money to help me with a
few "last hurrah" items and a couple of house
improvements.

—*PHIL MACKALL*
ARLINGTON, VIRGINIA
YEARS RETIRED: 1

IT'S HARD TO TELL HOW MUCH MONEY YOU'LL NEED TO RETIRE.
It's like making a bet on how long you'll live, which is a little
spooky. It's also been hard to let go of the part of me that
wants to make money. I've spent so much of my life thinking
about making money, to just let that go is not in my nature. I
appease myself with eBay. I find things at thrift stores and
estate sales and sell them on eBay. It's not much money,
hardly any, really, but it appeases the breadwinner in me.

—*R.R.*
CHARLESTON, WEST VIRGINIA
YEARS RETIRED: 1

FROM THE EXPERTS

FINANCIAL MATTERS: HOW MUCH DO YOU NEED?

There are two big financial questions you must answer for yourself: How much money do you need for retirement, and how much life insurance should you carry?

HOW MUCH DO YOU NEED FOR RETIREMENT?

Planners recommend anywhere from 70% up to 100% of pre-retirement income. Many people think that expenses decrease upon retirement. The fact is, however, that people maintain the same level of expenses they had prior to retirement—expenses generally don't begin to decrease until the eighth decade. One expense that increases during these years is health-care—particularly when you take into account the growth of alternative medical treatments (which usually are not covered by insurance).

In strategizing to have your funds last as long as you do, planners strongly caution against putting too much of your money in low-risk investments. Given longevity and the desire to offset the ravages of inflation, it is essential to maintain a portion of your investments in stock equity funds; probably a greater portion than you think. Most online retirement calculators allow you to input a pre-retirement and post-retirement rate of return for your investments, as well as an assumed inflation rate. Using one of these calculators, for most people, will be a sobering experience; you'll see the importance of increasing your savings.

MUST YOU HAVE LIFE INSURANCE?

When we say "life insurance," we mean having an appropriate policy in force, of the right size, to provide income for a surviving spouse and, in many cases, a legacy for children and grandchildren. It's critical to arrange some amount of permanent coverage, particularly when it comes to replacing lost income from the passing of a spouse. A typical scenario (without life insurance) would force the surviving spouse to live on half the income that was available. Although life insurance may be expensive if you wait too long, it offers a lump-sum amount to the family when they most need it and is still a solid way of leveraging your dollars. A financial adviser can help you figure out how much insurance and what kind of policy to buy: the point is, the earlier you purchase it, the less it costs throughout your lifetime.

Remember, the greatest gift we can give our kids is to visit without having to stay!

—**Craig Trojahn**
National Life and Financial Services Trainer
Farmers Insurance Group
Los Ranchos, New Mexico

DURING THE FIRST SIX MONTHS OR SO AFTER RETIREMENT,
I thought: Uh-oh, this is not working. It's really expensive. Dinners out every night, shopping, shows, travel—I think I just didn't know what to do with myself. After a while, I realized I could have as much fun inviting people over, or going to their homes. Dining can be cheap if I insist on value places to go. I need very few new clothes or furniture. So, in fact, life is very much within my means now. But it did take a while for me to calm down and figure out what's important.

—*JUDY CAPEL*
NEW YORK, NEW YORK
YEARS RETIRED: 3

WHEN IT COMES TO FINANCES I believe in a few simple rules:

1. Trust no one. Always get a second opinion on anything of substance.
2. If you love your family and value the relationships, do not give them power of attorney except for health care, and make all financial matters joint, you *and* son, not you *or* son. Money brings out the worst in everyone. Hire a lawyer if needed and make sure you have a health care living will and a will and trust.
3. Don't sign contracts with people unless *you* called them.
4. Limit what you buy from TV commercials.
5. If you must loan money to a family member, draw up a detailed written agreement stating what was borrowed and how and when it is to be paid back, signed and dated.

> —BARRY BIANCO
> BRISTOL, WISCONSIN
> YEARS RETIRED: 2

I WAS MOST CONCERNED WITH MONEY—how long the funds will last. Fortunately, I had a pretty sizable IRA, and then I put money into an SEP after I retired. That was the primary reason I kept consulting after retirement, so I'd have some money coming in.

> —BARRY MUNDT
> ASHEVILLE, NORTH CAROLINA
> YEARS RETIRED: 14

IT WAS IMPORTANT TO BE FINANCIALLY INDEPENDENT when I retired. I didn't want to worry about working. I didn't want to worry if my hobby made an income. For instance, photography is something I'm interested in, and if income comes from it, fine; but that's only in the back of my head. If it doesn't, then it continues as my hobby.

> —GARY SMITH
> SAN ANTONIO, TEXAS
> YEARS RETIRED: 1

DARK THOUGHTS

I GUESS IT'S NEVER TOO EARLY TO PLAN for your eventual demise; I'm told it's inevitable. My financial planner insisted I create a will right after my retirement was official. It seemed morbid to me and like something only an "old" person would do. But he told me that people of any age can make one and that if you have any real property you really should have one. He said that without it, you can't be sure what will happen to your assets after your death, and that in certain situations the government can even claim some of it. Well, that was all I needed to hear. I'd rather throw my stuff away than give it to the government. Get yourself a will.

—*EDNA STENZEL*
VIENNA, OHIO
YEARS RETIRED: 2

• • • • • • • • •

BE SURE TO LET YOUR FAMILY KNOW EXACTLY what your wishes are regarding your remains and your funeral. There is no such thing as being too specific; anything left unsaid will be decided by someone else. Even if you are alive, you may be incapacitated and unable to convey your wishes. Do it while you are still able.

—*R.M.*
BOARDMAN, OHIO
YEARS RETIRED: 2

• • • • • • • • •

WE'RE BOTH IN GREAT HEALTH, but we have had discussions as to what we should do when one of us passes on. The answer for both of us is that there should be no sadness, only celebration of the life that has passed. Then the living mate should find more joy in the rest of his/her life.

—*MARLENE MILLER*
TAMPA, FLORIDA

IF I'D HAD A CRYSTAL BALL AND KNOWN the market was going to tank, I would've paid for my mortgage. So, my only advice about money: Pay off your mortgage if you can!

> —*JUDY CAPEL*
> *NEW YORK, NEW YORK*
> *YEARS RETIRED: 3*

• • • • • • • •

YOU MOST LIKELY HAVE VERY CONSERVATIVE INVESTMENTS that pay next to no interest. Our daughter came to us and needed a large chunk of money to renovate a house. She guaranteed us a rate of return that was modest, but still more than the next-to-nothing interest we were earning in our safe accounts. Now, I would only recommend this if you absolutely know your kids are trustworthy—and even then we wrote up official documents just in case—but in our case it worked out wonderfully for all parties. My daughter got the money cheaper than from a bank (and let's face it, the bank didn't want to loan her that much anyway), and we got all of our money back with better interest than we were earning.

> —*MARY C.*
> *TUCSON, ARIZONA*

• • • • • • • •

THE KEY TO A FINANCIALLY SUCCESSFUL RETIREMENT is to be married to someone who has a J-O-B.

> —*PAULA*
> *VANCOUVER, B.C., CANADA*
> *YEARS RETIRED: 3*

• • • • • • • •

DON'T CARRY YOUR CREDIT CARD WITH YOU: that's number one. Number two: I ask myself, "Do I want this? Do I need this?" I usually answer, "No, I don't." And then I walk away.

> —*JOAN ALAGNA*
> *BROOKLYN, NEW YORK*
> *YEARS RETIRED: 2*

I WAS IN THE CAR ABOUT SEVEN YEARS AGO with my younger sister. She and her husband had just retired, and I'm thinking, "Why am I still working my buns off?" I said, "How can I retire?" and I pulled the car over and made her get out a pencil and some paper, and we began to write down all my assets and what they were worth. I've always been good with budgets, so we began to form one: She wrote down food, insurance, doctor bills, mortgages, and what they cost month-ly, then subtracted the mortgages (since I planned to sell my real estate company to pay off my house). And that moment, I finally realized, "Hey, I can do this." It took place in that car and from that day, I really planned. It took about a year to make it happen—to sell the business and pay off our home mortgage. Once the pressure of mortgage payments was gone, it was so easy.

—*BARBARA STEVENS*
GATLINBURG, TENNESSEE
YEARS RETIRED: 6

Love, Life, Friends: Relationships

Regardless of your status as single, married, or divorced; as a parent or as a child; as someone who has always made time for friendships or who would get around to having those one day; retirement changes relationships. Retirement, interestingly enough, happens around the time that you might be seriously evaluating or re-evaluating the investment you are making into the important relationships in your life. The chapters to this point have focused on you—what makes you tick in terms of your passion and purpose? How can you take premium care of your body and mind? Now it's time to explore those relationships that will enhance all of those experiences. And although ultimately the change is typically positive, it is often difficult.

For married couples, the rhythm of the relationship changes, and change is hard. You will hear from couples who "married for dinner but not for lunch," and needed to find their own way to determine a mutual schedule and expectations that work. For others, retirement has been a well-planned event that enables them to share projects and journeys that up to now have been only dreams.

Marriage and personal partnership have been something some people never made time for. It is interesting how often careers and years seem to fly by, leaving retirement as the perfect time to learn how to become, as one of my clients put it, "a co-pilot of my own life." If dating and meeting new people are part of your retirement experience, this chapter offers some advice that will help take some of the fear and anxiety out of the midlife-and-better dating experience. And we can't forget about sex! One of our experts addresses this touchy topic with sensitivity and optimism.

Others find that being part of the sandwich generation— those caring for both aging parents and for children (or grandchildren) at the same time—makes their retirement experience something they may not have planned for. Read on and learn from all those who experienced relationships in retirement in so many ways.

WHEN I FINALLY RETIRED, IT WAS DIFFICULT FOR BOTH OF US in the beginning. Since he had retired first, he came and went on his own. After I retired, I found myself questioning where he was going, what time he would be back, and so on. And if I sat down to do the crossword puzzle in the newspaper in the morning, he would ask me if I was "going to do anything" that day. That irritated me. It was my time to retire, and if I wanted to do the crossword puzzle, that was up to me! It took a while to adjust to being together so much of the time. I had to reinforce that the kitchen was my territory and I was the boss there. Often, he would come into the kitchen and ask what I was doing, why was I doing it that way, and so on. After a while, I would go down to his shop in the basement and ask what he was doing and why he was doing it that way! He soon got the message.

—*LINDA DIBERNARDO*
PORTSMOUTH, NEW HAMPSHIRE
YEARS RETIRED: 5

IF YOU HAVE A GOOD MARRIAGE, it's just delightful being around each other 24/7. But then, Jim has never alphabetized my spices. That happened to a friend of mine. It did not work: That husband was escorted out of the kitchen.

—*J.L.*
MINNEAPOLIS, MINNESOTA
YEARS RETIRED: 10

I WAS AFRAID THAT WHEN MY WIFE and I were forced to spend so much more time together than we were used to, it would lead to a lot more fights. But we've gotten along splendidly. I guess I worry too much. It helps that she takes one night a week to see the girls and I do a guys' night out just about every Friday.

—*BILL DAVIS*
STRUTHERS, OHIO

BE SELF-RELIANT. Try not to rely so much on the family. Retired people who rely on their family usually are disappointed. The young family members, no matter how much they love the old man, they have a thing about not being bothered too much. Be independent as much as possible. I rely on my family, but I have to keep aware that this is not a desirable thing.

—*RICHARD BING, M.D.*
PASADENA, CALIFORNIA
YEARS RETIRED: 3

* * * * * * * * *

BEING ABLE TO SPEND SOME TIME with your kids and their kids is the best part of being retired.

—*PATRICK CALIENDO*
POLAND, OHIO

* * * * * * * * *

WE BOUGHT SOME LAKESHORE PROPERTY NEARBY, which has allowed us to spend a lot of time with our kids and grandkids. When we were looking at property, we considered something in Arizona or Florida, but that would have meant spending less time with the grandkids, and we didn't want that. The grandkids see we all have fun, but there's also work to do. There are a lot of oak trees on the property, for example, so that's become a family activity: When it's too cold to go in the lake, the whole family rakes leaves.

—*ANONYMOUS*
WOODBURY, MINNESOTA
YEARS RETIRED: 9

* * * * * * * * *

I ALWAYS KIDDED WITH MY HUSBAND: "For better or worse, but not for lunch." If you're going to retire it doesn't mean I'm going to be with you 24 hours a day.

—*LIZ ALDERMAN*
WESTCHESTER COUNTY, NEW YORK

OUR RELATIONSHIP KEEPS GETTING BETTER. I can say the hardest time was in the earlier part of our careers. I was probably a pill to live with when I was just career-focused. As we have gotten older, we have just had this fabulous relationship. It has many different layers to it. Even after 25 years I think she is the hottest woman going. There is still plenty of romance happening in that relationship. It's a chapter of life less focused on "I" and more focused on "We." You are less concerned about your own career, less concerned about credit. When you get to this age you don't need an award. It's not I and I, it's We and We.

—*COREY GOODMAN*
MARSHALL, CALIFORNIA

• • • • • • • •

I HAVE A SEPARATE OFFICE that I can go to. That's the main reason our relationship has not changed.

—*ART KOFF*
CHICAGO, ILLINOIS
YEARS RETIRED: 8

• • • • • • • •

FAMILY TIME

Surveys confirm that many retirees find their most enjoyable activity to be spending more time with their adult children and grandchildren.

• • • • • • • •

MY HUSBAND AND I go on dates once a week to a movie or dinner. We call it date night, and in a restaurant we frequent they call us the "date-night couple."

—*SHIRLEY KELSO*
METHUEN, MASSACHUSETTS
YEARS RETIRED: 20

The Coach's Corner
DATING AT MIDLIFE: WHAT YOU NEED TO KNOW

When it comes to dating in midlife there seem to be two types of people: those who are like the proverbial kid having fun while looking for the pony in the pile of ... well, you know what; and those who consider it a necessary evil—or one to be avoided at all cost.

I'd like to propose that there is actually a middle ground and that the thought process and actions reflected in this middle ground will yield two important outcomes: enjoyment during (most of) the dating process and a higher probability of achieving the results you are looking for. Here's what you need to have in place to work from this middle ground:

Know thyself ... and get a quick read of others.
Did you know that you can tell a lot about a person if you know what section of the newspaper (for those of us who still read our papers rather than the online version) he or she picks up first? I should have known what I was in for when my soon-to-be husband consistently reached for two sections— sports and travel. That pretty well defines his passions. As for me, well, I guess I'm what you might call a closet romantic: people are always shocked to learn that the first section I reach for in Sunday's *New York Times* is invariably the weddings and engagements announcement section. I look for interesting stories, and guess what: They tend to be about people who marry in midlife or later. There are a few important things I've learned from my very unscientific survey:

- People are lovable (in the relationship/romantic sense) at any age.

- While the tendency is for men to look for women of a significantly younger vintage, there are plenty of men who are looking for someone around their own age. In fact, there are a growing number (in my anecdotal study) of couples where the woman is a few years older than her lover.
- With age comes clarity. As I read about what brought these couples together, it is almost always based on mutual interests and a deeply held sense of knowing, "This is the one."

So, perhaps the first question you ask a potential date might be: What section of the paper do you read first?

Don't put all of your eggs in one basket.
Recognize that dating is just one aspect of your life. Imagine for a moment that your life is made up of a portfolio of activities. Think about how you invest your time now; then reconsider how much time and energy you actually want to invest in each area of your life. As we age, we are more certain about who we are than earlier in life, where the focus was on who we wanted to become. Take that self-knowledge and look for another sage soul who shares your interests and passions. Look at relationships as a series of puzzle pieces making up the picture of your life. There are many different pieces in your puzzle: Take some of the pressure off by reminding yourself that a romantic relationship is just one piece.

Be thoughtful about re-entry into the dating world.
The biggest challenge associated with getting back out in the dating world typically has more to do with self-confidence than anything else. I like to encourage people to get into "game shape" for the dating experience. Do you feel and look your best? Need a new style? Take a visit to the make-up counter, hair stylist, or boutique and treat yourself in a way that makes you feel good about how you present yourself.

Are you getting enough sleep? Eating well? Exercising? Research has shown that those people who understand and pay attention to their physical, emotional, spiritual, and cognitive needs feel more energetic and report higher levels of happiness and life satisfaction. Carpe diem—the dating will follow!

Define a successful date.
We've all lived long enough to know that having high expectations of how people will act toward us and how we "should be" often leads to disappointment. It's no wonder many dates end on that note or something close to it. The secret to successful dating is to look at the entire experience with a light heart and to imagine that it is part of a grand experiment rather than a means to an end. Dates are simply potentials for connection. And we all want connection. Just don't go to that first date with hopes like: "This might be the one: He sounds perfect on paper and my friends say we're perfect for each other—I hope I don't screw this up!" What I do advise is to set your intention around finding out the following three things on your date:

- One thing you have in common (a hobby, past history, etc)
- One goofy thing about each other
- One thing you would like to learn more about him/her

A friend of mine recently tried this and reported back that it changed the whole dating experience for him—from anxious to enjoyable. Rather than focusing on how the date "should" be (How should I be? How should she be? Is this going well?), he felt as though he had something to do. This "scavenger hunt" of information can even be shared with a date: It takes the pressure off. Try it and let me know how it goes.

—B.W.

NOW THAT I AM RETIRED, I take care of my two grandsons three days a week. I couldn't bear to think of them going to day care. I enjoy having them around. I was working when my kids were growing up. It's nice to be able to relax and play with them.

—*DONNA HANAFIN*
NIXA, MISSOURI
YEARS RETIRED: 4

* * * * * * * *

WE HAVE NEIGHBORS IN THEIR 60S who were recently married, each with grown children and grandchildren. They went on their honeymoon right after the wedding. Literally the day they returned—and without any warning—the new bride's godchild (a great-niece of hers) was dropped on their doorstep, and they were named the sole custodians. So as retirees, they were plopped right back into the life of elementary schools, homework, sleepovers, kids! At times it's overwhelming, but we also see how much they are in love and how they make the best out of having a surprise family so late in life.

—*MARTY*
CHICAGO, ILLINOIS

* * * * * * * *

I HAVE SIX CHILDREN AND 11 GRANDCHILDREN, with more probably on the way. I love being around the grandchildren, and my kids often ask me to babysit them while they go out. But I have found that there are times when I have to say no to babysitting. At first I didn't want to upset my kids by turning them down. But I found that they are more understanding than I gave them credit for. They know Mom is not a spring chicken anymore. And I simply don't have the energy to chase the grandchildren around as much as I'd like. I think it's important to chip in and help out when you can, but you have to know your limitations.

—*EILEEN MCCARTHY*
PITTSBURGH, PENNSYLVANIA
YEARS RETIRED: 8

I LOVE TO SEE MY GRANDKIDS, and we have them over a lot. But sometimes I say, "Sure, we'll have them over, but not the whole day because I have a lot of errands to do." If I can't do it, I just say so. What are they going to do?

> —*JANET*
> *MINNEAPOLIS, MINNESOTA*
> *YEARS RETIRED: 10*

• • • • • • • •

IT'S GOOD TO HAVE FAMILY AROUND, but not necessary. Be on your own. You just can't depend on other people, whether relatives or friends, to handle your life for you. I still live life like I did in my 20s or 30s.

> —*BOB RICH*
> *CHARLOTTE, NORTH CAROLINA*
> *YEARS RETIRED: 4*

• • • • • • • •

NO MORE WATER COOLER!?

Loss of social connections at work is the most unforeseen challenge of retirement.

• • • • • • • •

IT IS A GOOD SYMBIOTIC RELATIONSHIP, now that I'm home for my teenage daughter. I gain by having the emotional connection, and she gains by having the constant support. For instance, she's in a school play, with rehearsals every day. The kids were expected to go home after school at 2 p.m. and come back at 5 p.m. And she also has started taking voice lessons in the afternoon to get ready for the play. How could she do all this without me around? Now that I can drive her, I get a feeling of really being there for her—and it's an excuse to spend some quality time together.

> —*FRED*
> *MILLER PLACE, NEW YORK*
> *YEARS RETIRED: 2*

OUR JOB AS PARENTS is not over once the kids are in college. As we live out the remainder of our lives, we are a huge teaching influence on young people. This is also part of the boomer experience. My kids have seen me move from an idea and a dream to creating something and staying committed to it. It's inspired both of them. My daughter ended up coming to a conference about finding your passion and what you can do about it or how can you make a difference in the world. She went back home, decided to quit her job, and joined AmeriCorps. She's now working for a major NGO. And my son, who was 19 at the time, has completely changed his life. He's now started a global program for young people and become an expert on multi-generational dialogue.

> —*MARCIA JAFFE*
> *SAUSALITO, CALIFORNIA/ BALI, INDONESIA*

SIX MONTHS BEFORE I RETIRED, we had been planning on selling our house and moving to Florida. At the time, my wife was complaining that we were never going to have grandchildren. I told her, "You know, when I retire, one daughter will tell us she's expecting, and another will tell us the following year." Sure enough, at my retirement party, our daughter stood up and said, "Dad doesn't know it yet, but he's going to be a grandfather." Eighteen months after that, she had another child, and our oldest daughter had one, too. We didn't wind up moving.

> —*GALEN R. REIL*
> *RICHMOND, VIRGINIA*
> *YEARS RETIRED: 5*

WHATEVER HAPPENED IN THE PAST with your children, forget it. Give it up. Even God can't change the past. What you have is now; have a relationship with your child. It's precious.

> —*JOAN ALAGNA*
> *BROOKLYN, NEW YORK*
> *YEARS RETIRED: 2*

FROM THE EXPERTS
SEX DOES *NOT* RETIRE!

Ah, retirement—the perfect time to revive your sex life! Time at last to look again at the old "scripts"—you know, all those explanations of how the world works that we always took to be true—that told you that sex is only for the young and beautiful. Time to create new expectations for being not just older, but sexually wiser and smarter.

When I retired and told friends I was going to teach mid- and later-life sex education, they loaded my e-mails with jokes and cartoons. The jokes were about disinterested husbands and ugly wives; the cartoons featured sagging breasts and limp penises. Apparently the idea of sex education for adults was only a laughing matter. But during the past 12 years, I've discovered just the opposite: People are bursting with questions about sex in later life. They want to know how to cope with the many changes of aging: changing bodies, changing relationships, even changing values. Unfortunately, for many of us, one of the most powerful of those aforementioned scripts insists we *not* talk (seriously) about sex. In fact, that's often the first place to start: It's important to talk to partners about our needs and feelings, to talk to physicians about medications that may impact sexual functioning, possibly even to talk to people who are facing familiar issues, such as disease, the loss of a partner, or balancing one's children's needs with that of a new relationship.

Of course, it's vital to begin by knowing the physical changes that can be expected. But research shows that relationship factors and mental health may be more important predictors of sexual well-being than physiological changes. The key is not to fall prey to negative expectations, but to explore the many ways that sex will change, and, with determination, can even improve, as you grow older.

The hundreds of questions I've collected during workshops reveal the urgent need for people to converse about relationships and ethical issues, beyond simply learning the facts. *Everyone* has questions:

"What can I expect to happen to me physically and psychologically in the next 20 years?"

"Where can I go to meet a man when the fear of AIDS is always present?"

"Is it okay to masturbate when you don't have the partner you had for 48 years?"

"How does a single female deal with a man's erectile dysfunction when he is not knowledgeable?"

"What about my hateful feelings from past relationships that prevent a loving relationship?"

"How soon is too soon in a new relationship?"

"How can I approach a sexual discussion with my spouse after our long period of silence?"

"Is there a 'G' spot and where is it?"

"Is there any hope for arousal when a spouse has lost physical attractiveness?"

"How do you overcome strict religious 'dos and don'ts' in a sexual relationship?"

The big question is, will you just live with your questions, or take the time to discover answers that can lead you to a happy and healthy sexual future?

—**Peggy Brick, M.Ed, CSE**
President, Consortium on Sexuality and Aging
Kennett Square, Pennsylvania

IF YOUR HUSBAND IS STILL INVOLVED with the world—maybe retired, or on committees, or actively working—coming home to a woman who only is talking about golf and tennis, well, it's a little boring. I think its good to start a whole new world for yourself and then bring him in.

> —DORE HAMMOND
> BEDFORD, WESTCHESTER COUNTY, NEW YORK

• • • • • • • •

MULTIGENERATIONAL HOUSEHOLDS

There are almost 6 million grandparents living in a household with grandchildren under 18 years old. 2.4 million of those grandparents serve as the head of the household and are responsible for their grandchildren.

• • • • • • • •

THE MOST SURPRISING THING ABOUT RETIREMENT is that my husband and I still like each other. Retirement can be a dangerous time for people who don't understand each other, or people who have different expectations and end up disappointed with each other. If you keep an open mind and remain flexible, you'll have a pretty good shot at it. But if you're going to want your life the way it was before retirement, with very little transition or changes, you're setting yourself up for disappointment.

> —CAROL GILLEN
> ASHEVILLE, NORTH CAROLINA
> YEARS RETIRED: 9

• • • • • • • •

IF YOU HAVE GOOD FRIENDS, they will always be good friends. I still have my friends from the Bronx from when I was two.

> —MORT SHEINMAN
> NEW YORK, NEW YORK
> YEARS RETIRED: 10

I AM INTERESTED IN A RELATIONSHIP but I very much treasure, relish, and enjoy my freedom and the ability to do what I want to do when I want to do it. I would like a companion to do some things with but I am not preoccupied with it. It's very hard to find.

—*Sylvia Brown*
Valley Village, California
Years retired: Less than 1

• • • • • • • •

WE ARE PRETTY ROMANTIC. We don't buy each other presents; the day-to-day things are much more important. No jewelry, no flowers; just things that seem, on the surface, trite, like humor and laughter. We support each other, and once the stress of raising children was gone, we could relax. We even work together.

—*Adrian*
Los Angeles, California
Years retired: 3

• • • • • • • •

ORGASM FOR THE ELDERLY is an oxygenator. And if you want to lose weight, you can do that, too.

—*Donna Sheehan*
Marshall, California

• • • • • • • •

AT THIS STAGE IN MY LIFE, forming relationships is a problem, not because of my age, but because moving often is a problem. It's very hard to make friends where you can get down to the level of intimacy and relaxation that you do with friends you've known since you were young and foolish. Now you meet people when you're old and cautious. It's more superficial now. Going through traumatic life experiences does create intimacy, but not as fast or as well as being young and foolish together does.

—*Peter*
Minneapolis, Minnesota

5 TIPS FOR BEING SEXUALLY WISER AND SMARTER AS YOU GROW OLDER

1. **Reexamine your old sexual scripts.** Do they apply to your life now? In fact, there's a good chance they never enhanced your sex life at all! Challenge the messages you received in your youth, as well as those you receive daily from youth-obsessed media and advertisers looking to sell an expensive and often ineffective quick fix.

2. **Try communicating!** Be brave! Break the silence barrier. Start talking with your partner(s), physicians and friends.

3. **Remember that sex is more than intercourse.** Discover how "outercourse"—non-penetrative sex—is "the opening shot in a long-term process of remodeling sexual norms and exploring sexual options." As sex therapist Marty Klein says, "When you forget about erections and lasting longer and just focus on having the time of your life ... things will fall into place!"

4. **Explore the many resources that can help revive your sex life:**

   • Search for a sex/couples workshop, or encourage your local senior center, academy, or religious group to develop one. (The teaching manual *Older, Wiser, Sexually Smarter: 30 Sex Ed Lessons for Adults Only* provides everything that's needed to create informative, fun, and interactive sessions.)

- Find a book that addresses your particular concerns or interests. (See www. sexualityandaging.com for an extensive bibliography.)
- Check out the variety of websites offering advice, films, and sex toys. (See especially www.sexsmartfilms.com, www.sexualhealth.com, or www.sinclairinstitute.com.)
- If you're really stuck, consider talking to a certified sex therapist. Visit www.aasect.org

5. **Laugh!** Enjoy the adventure of overcoming all the old myths about sex and aging!

—Peggy Brick, M.Ed, CSE
Consortium on Sexuality and Aging

WE DEFINITELY HAVE DIFFERENT STYLES. I like to get up and watch *The Today Show* while I drink coffee and look at the paper. Dick likes it quiet. So we have had to negotiate this a little. When Dick is around, I feel more like I have to be doing something productive. I think that is my problem, though, and not his. We have a big enough house that we don't really have to interact 24/7.

—*HELENE*
SALT LAKE CITY, UTAH
YEARS RETIRED: 2

• • • • • • • •

I STILL HAVE A 16-YEAR-OLD KID AROUND THE HOUSE, and my wife works full-time, so I've assumed a lot of the domestic things: cooking, food shopping, getting my kid to school, going to soccer games. I don't do windows and don't do housecleaning. Anyway, I like cooking and food shopping more than my wife does. It's been pretty easy.

—*M.R.*
SAN FRANCISCO, CALIFORNIA
YEARS RETIRED: 1

IT'S IMPORTANT TO HAVE FRIENDS OF ALL AGES. The other day, I wrote three sympathy cards and I thought, "I have to get younger friends!" It's really important to connect with younger people; I do it through church activities and the gym, and I try to keep in contact with people I used to work with who are a little bit younger than I am.

—*HARRIET SMITH*
SAN ANTONIO, TEXAS
YEARS RETIRED: 2

I SPEND A FAIR BIT OF TIME IN MY STUDY, writing, while my wife does a lot of charity work in a thrift shop. Consequently, we don't follow each other around all day wondering what to do next, which I think would have led to friction.

—*B.L.*
SAN JOSE, CALIFORNIA
YEARS RETIRED: 8

COMMUNICATION IS KEY

Married couples should sit down and discuss a plan for life after retirement that includes finances, household roles, and, especially, how much time they plan to spend together.

BEING TOGETHER 24/7 AFTER YEARS and years of his being gone all day or traveling a lot was the biggest challenge. Continue your life as you did before retirement occurred, but set some time to be together: reading time in the afternoon, cocktail time before dinner.

—*NOLA SMITH*
TAMPA, FLORIDA
YEARS RETIRED: 25

SOUND FAMILIAR?

Some common issues for folks in my age range are these:

1. Many of us are caretakers for parents whose financial situation is precarious; their vulnerability is ours. Uncertainty regarding their longevity and a need for resources is a major factor.

2. While some of my siblings are quite stable, with no likelihood of needing anything from me, a couple of others could get tricky. We have arranged for health insurance for one because, despite her age and risk factors, insurance was not a priority for her. Getting the insurance for her was for our benefit because we felt if she got sick, we would have to do something.

3. Getting children to an independent, secure situation is a gift. But it's not always easy to do.

I feel reasonably secure in terms of having the basics covered, all the financial management stuff. But it is the life crises from so many possible different directions that disturb me.

—ANONYMOUS
OMAHA, NEBRASKA

IT'S IMPORTANT FOR RETIRED COUPLES to have a little time away from each other occasionally. I like to go away for the weekend with my sisters. And I really don't want Bill to go to the grocery store with me and rush me. It's my own time. When I'm shopping, I want him to be out fishing or at home reading. You have to respect each other's space.

—BARBARA STEVENS
GATLINBURG, TENNESSEE
YEARS RETIRED: 6

I WAS NEVER A PERSON WHO ENJOYED BEING ALONE, so I welcomed the opportunity to spend more time with my spouse now that I was home every day. (And luckily she's a great cook and made me spectacular meals!)

—*ANONYMOUS*
TORONTO, ONTARIO
YEARS RETIRED: 10

• • • • • • • •

HUSBANDS CAN LEARN HOUSEHOLD CHORES, and wives can learn to do the business for the family. Remember, at some point, one of you will be doing all of it anyway. My wife had never had to even balance a checkbook. I took care of all business. On formally quitting daily work, I spent time showing her where various stocks and bonds were located and whom to contact, and explained our personal banking system, since we had several accounts. Sure enough, in the space of less than one year, I had two heart bypass operations. I was incapacitated. She had to take over all of our business and was able to do so.

—*J.L.*
DALLAS, TEXAS
YEARS RETIRED: 15

• • • • • • • •

WOMEN WHO WERE STAY-AT-HOME MOMS need to be prepared for major changes when their husbands retire. My husband always wanted to know what I was doing. He wanted to organize my day, and then reorganize it. The trick is to not tell him your plans!

—*MARY BRIGHT*
ALLENTOWN, PENNSYLVANIA
YEARS RETIRED: 10

• • • • • • • •

MAKE PLANS WITH OLD FRIENDS. Recently, the girls from my high school graduating class got together for a reunion. You have to do things like that just to keep excited about life.

—*JANET*
PARMA, OHIO
YEARS RETIRED: 3

OUR DECISION AT THE POINT OF RETIREMENT was that I wouldn't be with my husband 24/7, and we have kept to that. In terms of friends and activities, we have "yours," "mine," and "ours." That has worked perfectly. We usually have breakfast together and discuss plans for the day and menus. And we come back together at dinnertime, unless we have a joint activity planned in the middle of the day.

—F.M.
ERDENHEIM, PENNSYLVANIA
YEARS RETIRED: 14

SURVEY SAYS: YES WE CAN!

The first comprehensive national survey of sexual attitudes, behaviors, and problems among older adults in the United States has found that most people ages 57 to 85 think of sexuality as an important part of life and that the frequency of sexual activity, for those who are active, declines only slightly from the 50s to the early 70s. Data from the University of Chicago's National Social Life, Health and Aging Project (NSHAP), showed that many men and women remain sexually active well into their 70s and 80s.

IT'S VERY DIFFERENT TO BE TOGETHER 24 HOURS A DAY, seven days a week. She plays golf and loves gardening. I have a workbench in the garage and study multiple subjects that I'm curious about. But when we're both in the house, we have to learn how to respect each other. My wife and I listen to different radio stations; she likes talk radio and I prefer music. We listen with headphones if we are in the same room and want to have it on.

—FRANK HAWK
LAKELAND, FLORIDA
YEARS RETIRED: 3

FROM THE EXPERTS

OVER 50 AND DATING (ONLINE)?

Dating is not something that gets easier with age. Whether you are coming out of a stable, long-term relationship or still looking for the right one, the challenges can seem overwhelming. "All of my friends are married—where can I find someone to date?" "I lead a busy life—how can I find the time?" "What would my children think of my seeing someone other than their mother/father?"

Once upon a time, challenges like these often kept older singles from searching for a great relationship. But the Internet has changed the way people search, meet, and fall in love. It can be a great tool to find someone special.

Internet dating and matchmaking sites have given people access to hundreds—even thousands—of potential partners who are also looking for love. And almost all dating sites offer more than just a name and a phone number or e-mail address. They also give users the chance to show their interests, passions, and ideals through their profiles. Some sites, like eHarmony, go even further. They use research and science to help determine which potential partners are the most compatible. These sites can give you a better chance of finding the right one. These days, matchmaking doesn't depend on what your friends think; it is based upon research on thousands of married couples.

If you decide to search for love on the Internet there are several important things to keep in mind.

- **Decide on your relationship goals.** Different Internet sites focus on different goals. Some are there for finding dates, others for finding friends, and others for finding long-term relationships. Before you join, learn what that site is known for and make sure it offers what you want.

- **Educate yourself about the process.** When you decide on a site to join, spend some time learning about the features. Many sites help you get to know other users through ice-breakers, secure e-mail, and even secure phone calling. All of these features can help you get to know someone before you ever meet in person.

- **Be patient.** It can take time to find a good relationship, and sometimes we forget that. So don't worry if you don't find someone in the first week or the first month, or even the first three months. If you do find that special someone it will be well worth the wait.

- **Use what you know.** A lifetime of relationships brings great wisdom. You know what made your past relationships great, and what made them not so great. Use those lessons when you are searching for someone new.

- **Keep your wits about you.** Keep safety in mind when dating, both online and offline. Unfortunately there are always fraudsters, sham artists, and unstable individuals whom you need to avoid. Almost every online dating site will have safety tips that you should read and keep in mind.

- **Have fun.** Dating should be fun. Even if you haven't found that special someone, you can get to know many new people, find some friends, and have a lot of good nights out.

Dating in your 50s, 60s, 70s, 80s (and even your 90s) is not only possible, but because of the Internet, is very popular. Many are trying it and finding great relationships.

—**Gian Gonzaga, Ph.D**
Senior Director of Research and Development
eHarmony.com
Pasadena, California

MAKE SURE YOU HAVE HUMAN INTERACTION EVERY DAY. I remember when I had children and I was in the house away from work, it was hard. Retirement is similar, especially if you're not married. I was very lucky when I retired; my grandson was starting university in my town, and he actually lived with me for a while. I still see him a lot. But mainly I see friends. I make sure there's a reason to get up and shower.

> —*G.H.*
> *CHAPEL HILL, NORTH CAROLINA*
> *YEARS RETIRED: 2*

• • • • • • • •

HAVING TO ADJUST TO YOUR SPOUSE is something many retirees may not expect. Sure, you've lived with them all these years, but through the years, they change; they aren't the same person you married. In fact, you've both changed, and you come home and find out you're both so different than you thought you were. You've got to have time to yourself; you've got to have freedom.

> —*DEE EYRE*
> *JACKSONVILLE, TEXAS*
> *YEARS RETIRED: 6*

• • • • • • • •

BETTER TOGETHER

Research shows that married couples are happier if they retire at about the same time.

• • • • • • • •

I LOST SOME OF MY SEXUAL DRIVE because I didn't have sex. The two things sex gives is that sense of intimacy and the romance. But the intimacy is so important in long-term relationships. And my partner whistles all week; it puts him in a great mood and he will do almost anything for me.

> —*DONNA SHEEHAN*
> *MARSHALL, CALIFORNIA*

IF I START TO GET ON HER NERVES, I just go for a walk.

—*TERRY HARRINGTON*
CUMBERLAND, MARYLAND
YEARS RETIRED: 2

• • • • • • • •

I BOWL WEDNESDAY NIGHTS and she bowls on Thursdays. We could bowl together, but this way we get a little break.

—*WALT BULLOCK*
BARRELVILLE, MARYLAND
YEARS RETIRED: 2

• • • • • • • •

I HAVE THE GREATEST HUSBAND IN THE WORLD, but too much time together can drive you crazy. At some point in your day, take quiet time alone. You need your own space.

—*MOLLY KOLB*
JACKSONVILLE, TEXAS
YEARS RETIRED: 10

• • • • • • • •

YOU'LL FIGURE OUT SOMETHING TO DO with your time. And if you don't, then your wife will find something for you.

—*BARNEY WISTROM*
LAVALE, MARYLAND
YEARS RETIRED: 6

• • • • • • • •

THE BIGGEST CHANGE SINCE I RETIRED IS THAT I get up later in the morning, and I spend time visiting with my wife, which we never did when we worked.

—*JOSEPH EMIL VUCINOVICH*
REDMOND, WASHINGTON
YEARS RETIRED: 7

• • • • • • • •

SOMEONE ONCE SAID HAVING YOUR HUSBAND retire is like having twice as much husband and half as much money.

—*SUSAN*
TAYLOR, TEXAS
YEARS RETIRED: 3

TIPS FROM A RETIRED EXECUTIVE

AMAZINGLY, HOUSEWIVES SPEND A LOT OF TIME out of the house. And while she is engaged with shopping, groceries, shopping, laundry/cleaning, shopping, and other errands, with careful planning you can have the whole house to yourself! However, it's best for both of you if you keep an "office," either an executive suite with a cubicle and steno-copier service, or stake out a corner at Starbucks or Barnes & Noble. Remember, she took you "for life," but not for lunch every day.

A good idea is to plan a meeting for lunch with her on a regular basis. It will be fun to do it, and both of you can avoid any feelings of guilt or abandonment. If you really want to be a hero, I suggest you plan, buy for, and pre-pare the evening meal once a week. The fact is, she is sick of second-guessing your tastes and figuring out what to do each day, and since you are retired, she doesn't have that "break" of a business dinner every once in a while, when she can just make a TV dinner for herself.

> —*T.S.*
> *TAMPA, FLORIDA*
> *YEARS RETIRED: 12*

YOU HAVE TO REMEMBER YOUR ROLE AS GRANDPARENT, and it is *not* to be involved in the kids' lives every day. My son and his wife live in Michigan, and I try to see them as often as I can without becoming a nuisance. They come in for Easter and Christmas, and I usually go out there for a week in the sum-mer. I think it's nice to be somewhat close but not too close. They need their space, too, so that they can raise their family.

> —*ELLEN WAYNE*
> *BOARDMAN, OHIO*

I WENT ON EHARMONY, I did Match.com, I did CatholicMatch.com. There's even a website for Italian-American singles. I've gone on dates. I always meet the man in a diner, in a public place. I went on perfectmatch.com and filled out a psychological profile—such crap—and I ended up having an 80-year-old professor wanting to meet me. What am I supposed to do with an 80-year-old professor? I like a guy who's physically active and likes to do things. When you're younger, you're drawn by looks. Now as an older adult, I look for a man who's well groomed: A man who shaves, and if he has a mustache or beard he keeps it trimmed. I look for a man who's not fat. Men are not supposed to be fat. I like thin men. He doesn't have to be highly educated. I base intelligence on a man's life experience. I also like someone who is very sensitive and open.

—JOAN ALAGNA
BROOKLYN, NEW YORK
YEARS RETIRED: 2

* * * * * * * *

THE RELATIONSHIPS HAVE MORE to do with aging than with retirement, I think. We've been married 24 years, but a lot of people our age have been married 45 years. Then there are people our age married two years, and they do seem to be kind of ... fluttery.

—PAULA
VANCOUVER, B.C., CANADA
YEARS RETIRED: 3

* * * * * * * *

AS I HAVE GOTTEN OLDER the pressure is off to not have to impress anybody; and how wonderful it is not to expect women to be attracted to me; and how wonderful it is when women are pleasant and line up around me, or hug me. Maybe it's because I am less "dangerous" then I was. As you get older, you are less of a threat.

—PAUL REFFELL
MARSHALL, CALIFORNIA

CLOSE ENCOUNTERS: LOVE IN THE THIRD AGE

ONE OF THE BEST THINGS ABOUT RETIREMENT is that it leaves you plenty of time to focus on the "fine points" of romance that sometimes get neglected when you're bogged down with work. My husband and I make sure to hold hands, sit close to each other, and make eye contact across a crowded room. He takes care of me when I'm sick, gets me a glass of wine, or goes to the store to buy me popcorn. We always say "please" and "thank you" and avoid criticizing each other. After 48 years together, our relationship is better than ever!

> —*GAY*
> *DENVER, COLORADO*

• • • • • • • • •

NOTHING WILL REVIVE YOUR SEX LIFE like being home all day, every day, with your spouse. It's like the period right after you first get married all over again.

> —*CARL COOKE*
> *CUMBERLAND, MARYLAND*
> *YEARS RETIRED: 1*

• • • • • • • • •

IT WAS HARD TO RETIRE BECAUSE AFTER MY DIVORCE, about halfway through my career, my work was really my life. But slowly I realized that I had been using my work to hide from the world. There were really very few social opportunities at work. Many of the women were younger than me, and there was no room for romance in my life. Soon after I retired, I joined a book club, which is where I met my husband. He has brought me so much happiness, and I'm so glad that I decided to stop working and explore life a little, even if I was scared and didn't know where it would take me. I guess I can thank my arthritis for something!

> —*BETTY*
> *DURHAM, NORTH CAROLINA*
> *YEARS RETIRED: 8*

PEOPLE ON THE VERGE OF RETIREMENT will be pleasantly surprised to find that once you retire and you both have unlimited time for each other again, you will quickly and easily fall into those old habits of trying to please each other again. If you never fell out of love in the first place, then it has always been there anyway. It's more often the lack of time that keeps you from realizing it. My advice is to just be there and spend time with each other. Enjoy the time you have together.

—*J.E.*
MORGANTOWN, WEST VIRGINIA
YEARS RETIRED: 2

DATING OLDER MEN CAN BE REALLY HARD. For example, the ordinary retired guy wants a woman to be really good-looking and physically to be in really great shape. But most men my age don't take care of themselves the way they expect women to. I give most of them a pretty low grade. And most men just want to stay home and watch TV, or they want to come over to my house and watch TV. But for most older women today, the whole world is exciting. We don't want to take care of some boring old man. For example, this older man called me, and we went out one time, and he's called several times since, and then he was mad because I hadn't called back, and finally I just told him, "Look, figure it out. I've been divorced since 1973—do you really think I want a relationship? I have my family, my job, and I need time for myself." I'm independent and I like it that way.

—*ANONYMOUS*
SEATTLE, WASHINGTON
YEARS RETIRED: 5

IF YOU ARE LUCKY ENOUGH TO FALL IN LOVE at this point in your life, don't play around. You don't have the time to waste like you once did. Tell her how you feel. I met my second wife on May 13. We were married three months later, in August.

—*M.K.*
GREEN MOUNT, VIRGINIA

SOMEONE ONCE ASKED ME, "What is the secret to a successful marriage?" I told him, sleep naked and every morning, give each other a hug and a kiss. We have done this for the last 30 years.

> —JULE
> SAN RAFAEL, CALIFORNIA

• • • • • • • •

THE STEREOTYPE OF MARRIAGE is where people have a long relationship and one spouse's domain was the home. Suddenly the outside person retires and is at home. But in our situation things weren't that clear-cut. During our marriage it went back and forth, so we're just at another one of these points. It's just as likely that I'll pick him up at the station after a long day of work and he'd be the one to come home and make dinner.

> —PAULA
> VANCOUVER, B.C., CANADA
> YEARS RETIRED: 3

• • • • • • • •

MY SISTER AND I ARE GETTING TO BOND NOW. I'm going to be moving into a new house near her, and until I can get in there, she's taken me in for a few months. We've never lived under the same roof since who knows when! So far, so good.

> —J.L.
> JACKSON, NEW JERSEY
> YEARS RETIRED: 2

• • • • • • • •

SEX IS EASIER AS YOU GET OLDER. There is less responsibility and there is less fear. You are more sure of yourself and you have done most of the things you wanted to do in life. In my case I have had a wonderful life doing all kinds of stuff. I don't have to put on the display that young guys do. As you get older, if you can retain your sense of humor about yourself and about sex and about life, that's the secret.

> —PAUL REFFELL
> MARSHALL, CALIFORNIA

MY WIFE WAS PANICKED. She was afraid that I would follow her around the house all day giving her ideas on how to run the house better. Her condition of my retirement was that I had to get an office or go to an office each morning. I would have breakfast, kiss her goodbye, and go to a small office in our town where I worked on volunteer projects, did some tutoring of high school students, or whatever. I sometimes spent an hour and went to play golf, or I might work all day.

—C. WILLIAM JONES
EASTON, MARYLAND

* * * * * * * *

KEEP CONNECTIONS WHERE YOU'VE BEEN and make new connections as individuals and as a couple. We have "our" friends, she has "her" friends, and I have "my" friends. That's good.

—GARY SMITH
SAN ANTONIO, TEXAS
YEARS RETIRED: 1

* * * * * * * *

I BASICALLY TOOK OVER THE HOUSEWORK, so that when she came home there was nothing for her to do. Her job became easier because she knew that she didn't have to do the vacuuming and waste weekends on chores. There are no sexist roles here: Why can't I pick up a mop? Being retired, it's my time to take care of the fort.

—MICHAEL
SAYVILLE, NEW YORK
YEARS RETIRED: 1

* * * * * * * *

IF MY HUSBAND ASKS ME ONE MORE TIME where I am going when I get up from the couch, I am going to have to kill him. Seriously, when both partners retire you have to create a balance of time together, time apart, and socialization. You have to do this with intent.

—CECELIA WRAY
ATLANTA, GEORGIA
YEARS RETIRED: LESS THAN 1

A LOT OF PEOPLE DON'T CONSIDER BEING with older people; they consider age a barrier. I never did. I can still see an attractive man looking attractive. In fact I thought my eye surgeon was gorgeous! He looked like an Italian movie star. He was so charming and I thought, Oh, god. He was maybe in his late 50s, but I am too old for him. You know I really don't want to get involved anymore. Twice is enough. I can't stand another loss.

—*SUE SIEGAL*
SAN FRANCISCO, CALIFORNIA

• • • • • • • •

IF YOU MEET THE RIGHT PERSON, your sexual and emotional life blends together.

—*STEVEN WERLIN*
DILLON BEACH, CALIFORNIA
YEARS RETIRED: 3

• • • • • • • •

WHEN I HAD SMALL CHILDREN, my focus was on family things, although I was working. All the decisions I made were family-first. Then there was a period where it was more just about the couple. Then suddenly, the family became more primary again: older parents, health issues, the death of one parent. Then my children moved near me and had grandchildren, and my father moved near me. I never expected this: I'd moved far away from my family, didn't grow up near grandparents, so it seems weird to have four generations living in the same town. It certainly takes a bunch of time. But I feel lucky and I love it. It's a pleasure.

—*PAULA*
VANCOUVER, B.C., CANADA
YEARS RETIRED: 3

• • • • • • • •

HOLDING HANDS AND BIG HUGS AREN'T TOO BAD. I try to kid her out of her seriousness. We go out for breakfast every morning, to get out of the house.

—*JIM*
MORTON, ILLINOIS
YEARS RETIRED: 17

IT'S A GREAT COMFORT TO HAVE MADE YOUR PEACE. Mend fences. And have a circle of friends and—if you're lucky—family, and colleagues. I'm terribly sorry for people who go through life alone in retirement, and it can happen. It's more important to have a good relationship than to be right.

—SUZIE
SAN RAFAEL, CALIFORNIA
YEARS RETIRED: 3

· · · · · · · ·

REMEMBER THAT SEX IS THE SPORT of the elderly for two main reasons: You do it lying down; and it is really good slow!

—CINDY JOSEPH
NEW YORK, NEW YORK

· · · · · · · ·

IF YOU ARE IN A RELATIONSHIP, don't fall into the trap of putting off sex because you don't have time, or because of the kids, or you've got to fix the car. You always must make time, even if you have to make an appointment, once a week at least, to have intimacy with your partner. Sunday sex is one of our goals. Sunday morning, nobody calls us before noon. No matter how we feel when we wake up; no matter if we had a late night, or haven't slept, or whatever. We have a cup of coffee and we have a nibble on a banana or something light and we just begin to cuddle. And once you begin to cuddle all kinds of things happen; pretty soon you are in the mood. And we benefit all week. It's very healthy for you.

—PAUL REFFELL
MARSHALL, CALIFORNIA

Just Click: Technology

A chapter about technology in a book about retirement? How crazy is that? In fact, it's crazy not to think about it. Today, those over 50 are the fastest growing age group to use social networking as a way to expand connections and stay in touch with family and friends. More and more people are using digital technology for planning their trips, researching an impending move, studying the job market, finding recipes, and better understanding the resources available to caregivers. Here's an interesting tidbit: Whether or not they meant to do so, the iPad was created in just the right size for "older" eyes. Initial sales to those aged 50 and over were well beyond anything anticipated.

As you'll read in this chapter, technology makes the world a smaller place. One of our interviewees met a man in Indonesia, helped that man launch a business, and now is able to remain involved and up to date about his progress! Are you traveling too much to keep up with local news? The Internet is a perfect way to check your favorite news sources while on the go.

*The challenge is to have technology be a useful and effi-
cient tool for you without becoming a slave to it. Once you
become proficient with Internet searches and e-mail it's
easy, some might say, it is dangerously alluring, to spend an
inordinate amount of time there. So click away now and
then and keep in touch the old-fashioned way!*

I WORK WITH PEOPLE IN APPALACHIA who don't have deeds to their properties— they have royal charters. They have had the same property for 300 years. They have a sense of place I will never experience. But they have been victimized by globalization. They abandoned farming 100 years ago and worked in textiles which offered a better life, but textiles went to China. They were caught in bubble of history that burst. My role is to show them how to get back to what they were doing 100 years ago in farming. We use the Internet to help them to sell their product. For the uninitiated, it's about selling food. For the initiated, it's about giving the people the hope they can have a job by using their farmland to practice high-intensity, sustainable agriculture. The ones who get it say, "Ah, it is a way for rural people to use and understand broadband, thus bringing them into the 21st century." We can open an Internet avenue to increase their skills and for all the rest it has to offer. It looks like we are selling food but we are really connecting people into the 21st century.

—*TIM WILL*
RUTHERFORD COUNTY, NORTH CAROLINA
YEARS RETIRED: NOYB

• • • • • • • •

I HAVE BEEN USING THE INTERNET for a long time. But we (my husband and I) are really slow at using the cell phone; we never turn it on. Our kids get really mad. We only use it to find each other at Walmart.

—*SUE*
SAN RAFAEL, CALIFORNIA
YEARS RETIRED: 16

• • • • • • • •

I AM NOT ENTIRELY CLEVER with computers and that makes me mad at myself: I don't like to feel inept. Its one of those things I might do something about. I want to buy an iPad for reading because you can light up the screen. I am determined to learn to use an iPhone because I love all the features on it. But that's on my back burner; it's solitary and doesn't involve people, and I like people a lot.

—*SUE SIEGAL*
SAN FRANCISCO, CALIFORNIA

SOMEONE SAID TO ME, "Oh, you were raised with primitive communication. You had the telephone and the postal service." You know what? She was right. That was primitive communication.

—*LINDA AMSTER*
NEW YORK, NEW YORK
YEARS RETIRED: 5

• • • • • • • •

ONLINE PRESENCE

The number of older adults actively using the Internet has increased significantly in recent years. Among adults 65-plus, the increase in the number of women using the Internet has exceeded the increase of men by six percentage points. This group spends an average of 58 hours a month online.

For 89%, checking their personal e-mail was their number-one online activity. Viewing or printing maps and checking the weather were the second and third most popular online activities, with 69% and 60%, respectively.

• • • • • • • •

USE THE COMPUTER TO STAY IN TOUCH. One of my boys is local, but the other is not. I have found that with computer innovations like the Internet, e-mail, and digital photos, I can stay in touch with them much more easily than my parents could with me when I left home. My son sends me photos of his kids in an e-mail about once a week so I can really see how they are growing. It does make me feel closer to them.

—*RAY BALLAST*
BOARDMAN, OHIO

YOU CAN WASTE A WHOLE LOT OF TIME on the Internet. But e-mail is great for keeping in touch with people near and far. I'm more in touch with people than when I had to write letters!

> —*SUZIE*
> *SAN RAFAEL, CALIFORNIA*
> *YEARS RETIRED: 3*

* * * * * * * *

SOCIAL MEDIA HAS JUST TAKEN OFF in the last couple of years. I keep my personal and professional accounts separate. I am able to follow the nieces and nephews on Twitter; that's how I know where the kids are. Lets face it, twentysomething nieces and nephews are not going to call their uncles and aunts to say, This is what I am doing. They've got lives to lead. My non-personal Twitter account is business-related, but my clients who are my age do not Twitter. My generation does not get Twitter at all. I don't think the younger generation appreciates how valuable privacy is. On Facebook, people put up their breakfast menu; who bloody well cares? You will never know what I had for breakfast on Facebook.

> —*BERYN HAMMIL*
> *SAN FRANCISCO BAY AREA, CALIFORNIA*

* * * * * * * *

I'M SORT OF A LUDDITE, but when I think something is useful to me, I do it. I treat it exactly the same way I treat the automobile. I've been driving since I was 17. Many people have tried to explain the internal combustion engine to me. I don't get it, but I can still drive a car. Same with computers: I have no idea how they work, and I'm not interested in knowing how, but I like to be able to do what I need to do. At the radio station there's an engineer who wants to explain to me about the satellite and tower. I say, just show me which button to push. It's a somewhat old-fashioned technology, but it's new to me. I enjoyed the adrenaline rush of not being certain I knew how to do it. I'm going to get an iPhone, but other than that, I'm not much interested in playing technology.

> —*PAULA*
> *VANCOUVER, B.C., CANADA*
> *YEARS RETIRED: 3*

FROM THE EXPERTS

A DAY IN THE LIFE OF A JETSON KID

My dad brought home our first television in 1955. It was black and white and had a very small screen by today's standards, but when he plugged it in and turned it on, I was hooked for life. There was not much programming back then—mostly news and a few dramas—but that glowing screen grabbing pictures out of thin air was pure magic. That one device imbued a generation of kids my age with a lifelong love for electronic gadgets of all kinds.

As TV programming evolved, one could find most of my generation cross–legged in front of the tube, lost in the futuristic world of the Jetsons. We were living a fantasy life in an "ultra-smart" home, complete with flying cars, household robots, and flat-screen video telephones. It didn't stop there: as teenagers, we rode with the crew of the U.S.S. Enterprise, hoping we'd be using that wireless communicator device in our lifetime.

We are not kids anymore, and some of us are even considering retirement. But we are the first generation to grow up watching television. We are the generation that designed and developed cutting-edge information technologies like the Internet, the Web, computers, and cell phones; the innovations that have changed our lives in large and small ways, especially transforming the way we stay connected during our days. So now that we're arrived at the 21st century, what is a typical day like for a plugged-in baby boomer?

We wake up in the morning to the sweet smell of coffee, having programmed the "smart" percolator the night before.

With a warm cup in hand, we sit down at a computer to check the morning's e-mails and get local news and world headlines from any number of reputable news outlets, now online. Hometown news is just a Google search away: No wonder paperboys on bicycles are out of work.

Remember picking up the telephone to eavesdrop on local gossip on the party line? Today's party line is your social network of choice; perhaps Facebook, Twitter, or MySpace. You follow conversations among friends, see pictures of the grandchildren from the past weekend, or read a distant cousin's latest political rants. Since social networking became popular, have you noticed that people circulate fewer jokes and more YouTube video links?

Exercise is an important aspect of a boomer's daily life, and these days, we clip an electronic pedometer to our waistbands before taking our daily walk around the block,. When we get home, we use a USB connector to download our daily step count to the computer. This smart little gadget sorts out aerobic vs. passive steps and displays a chart of how effectively we've exercised today, this week, last month, and even last year. With our USB-enabled blood-pressure cuff we can compare our blood pressure to our activity to see if daily exercise is having beneficial effects. Step on the wireless scales and it sends data to the same computerized chart for an even more complete picture. Tracking our health on several levels at once, in one place, can be crucial for those of us managing a chronic or age-related weight or diabetic condition.

While we walk, our smart phone entertains us with our favorite tunes or a new audio book. And when we're on the move, we use our smart phone to call up a street map of whatever town we're in to find shopping, a place for lunch, or the nearest clean restroom.

Back home, inexpensive wireless routers bring the Internet to all corners of our houses, allowing online movies to be streamed to high-definition, flat-screen televisions hanging on the walls. Webcams monitor the interiors; we can watch our cat prowling the empty house when we're away. Robots vacuum our floors. Mobile phone coverage is worldwide, and more and more societies are joining the wireless way of life. Remember those Star Trek communicators we coveted? Nowadays, it's no problem to talk to friends and family across the world by flipping open a laptop and setting up a face-to-face video chat. The Jetson home has almost become reality during our lifetime.

The Jetson kids may be aging, but don't expect them to "retire." Instead, watch them "re-wire," embracing new technologies with zeal. They are comfortable with technology, and are part of the increasing demand for connectivity devices—smarter smart phones, more and better quality online video, to name a few. Many boomers feel that keeping on top of new technologies will be the key to remaining connected and independent as they age. They will be the first generation to reconsider aging, continuing to follow the development of the computer age they once dreamed of, rather than letting it pass them by.

—Susan Ayers Walker, BSEE/MSCS
Journalist and Managing Director
SmartSilvers Alliance
Atherton, California

I LIKE E-MAIL AND HAVE SEVERAL FRIENDS that exchange jokes/stories. I do research on stocks I am considering selling or buying. I often use the Internet to look up answers to any questions I have. I can get better buys on some things I need. I can review comments of other owners of certain products to have an idea of their reliability. I can get answers quickly through e-mail. When getting ready to travel, I look up info/prices on motels, and info about the locations we are headed to. I know there is a lot of baloney out there, but you just have to sort through it and try to use credible sources.

—*JIM*
MORTON, ILLINOIS
YEARS RETIRED: 17

• • • • • • • •

BEFORE ALL THIS TECHNOLOGY CAME IN, you were really cut off from the world if you stayed home, and now, even at my age, I have a website, a Twitter account, and a blog. Once you get out there it just keeps growing. It's such a resource. I keep saying to my mother, who is 85, I'll go with you to the library and show you how to set up an e-mail account so I can send you pictures of your grandkids. She says no. I say, You're missing out. Don't be scared. If you are housebound, your whole world opens up.

—*DORE HAMMOND*
BEDFORD, WESTCHESTER COUNTY, NEW YORK

• • • • • • • •

WITH TECHNOLOGY I AM UNTETHERED from my desk. I can respond to clients' phone calls; I can source materials from wherever I am in the world. I was on a beach in Hawaii and I got a call from potential client. She said, How will I know if I take you on that I will always reach you? And I said, Case in point, I am on the beach in Hawaii and you got me. That's how accessible I am.

—*BERYN HAMMIL*
SAN FRANCISCO BAY AREA, CALIFORNIA

I HAVE TO USE A COMPUTER, and I did use it at work all the time. But it just isn't a natural thing for me. I came to it at 70 years old when my husband got a computer. Finally I said, show me what it's all about. And so I am going to take a computer class. I do a lot of word processing, but I do need to know more. I do e-mail, but getting a plane ticket? Somehow, that doesn't work. So I call them up and pay 10 dollars more.

—*SYLVIA BROWN*
VALLEY VILLAGE, CALIFORNIA
YEARS RETIRED: LESS THAN 1

I AM AN INTERIOR DESIGNER and a lot of my clients live in senior residences; I help them downsize and make their new home just as lovely as the one they left. A lot of the people living in senior homes are adapters of technology. They have embraced it with both hands. Some have access to cars and are out; some are not, but they still have access to what is out there, simply by turning on their laptops. I have a friend who bought an iPad; she's 70 years old, widowed, never had a computer, knows how to type but didn't even know what a hyperlink was. We got her on an iPad with a keyboard. And every week she is learning more and more. She e-mails her family, does research, and shops online.

—*BERYN HAMMIL*
SAN FRANCISCO BAY AREA, CALIFORNIA

PLAYING COMPUTER GAMES IS A PASSION. I love the ones that you can download and play for free. They mostly have limitations that you can only play them for a period of time or only play them a couple of times for free. It doesn't really matter to me if I end the game; I just like playing them. I play them to keep my mind active.

—*CECELIA WRAY*
ATLANTA, GEORGIA
YEARS RETIRED: LESS THAN 1

MY GRANDCHILDREN ARE ALL ON FACEBOOK and texting on their cell phones. I think that's the way they spend their day! I prefer e-mail that is more personal, and talking on the cell phone.

—*B.D.*
SEATTLE, WASHINGTON
YEARS RETIRED: 18

• • • • • • • •

THE INTERNET IS A GREAT THING. I use it every day. I have all my friends on there, I chat, I'm on Facebook. I take a photography class online. Facebook is how I keep track of my young friends. Make sure you get on Facebook, and don't be afraid of it because it's a great way to keep up with your friends' grandchildren, your grandchildren. You see all of these people and you say, "Look what he's doing!" It's like traveling. Older people are scared of Facebook. My brother, who is three years older, said, "I don't want none of that." I said, "What do you mean? It's just like the newspaper, the TV. It's something that is there; you don't have to go there every day. It's like the newspaper. You open it and read what you like.

—*MILAGROS BETHARTE*
BRONX, NEW YORK
YEARS RETIRED: 3

• • • • • • • •

I COULD MAKE A CASE THAT the most important factor in my career change (away from being a general contractor toward being an editor and writer) was the computer. I'd been a writer before, but it was very difficult to complete anything because of my typing and rewriting skills and habits. Word processing changed all that. It's possible to continually rewrite, improve, and process text, and it's not a giant mess. Word processing made it possible to be a professional writer and editor. And as a grant writer, I will go online to educate myself about medical procedures and come up with something that can be reviewed by my experts, in order to get to a document we can use for the grant applicaton. The Internet has profoundly changed the nature of my job.

—*PETER*
MINNEAPOLIS, MINNESOTA

5 TIPS FOR MASTERING ELECTRONIC MAIL

Nowadays, e-mail has all but replaced "snail mail" in most areas of life. Although people still appreciate receiving a holiday card or exotic postcard, they expect to get in touch with you electronically, and assume you're able to reply in kind. Don't let them down! E-mail is your best bet to keep in touch with old friends and far-away family, connect with the younger generation, keep up a social life even if you're physically limited or isolated, and be prepared for new jobs and volunteer opportunities. You might be a fabulous writer of letters both formal and informal, but e-mail etiquette is not exactly the same. Learning the new rules of e-mail will show the world that you're no millennial novice.

1. **Answer Promptly.** The instantaneous nature of e-mailing has cut down acceptable response times to practically nothing. If you receive an e-mail, particularly from an organization or business you want to be involved with, you're expected to get back to them right away. Delaying your response might make you appear nonchalant, or worse, uncomfortable with technology, so hop to it! It *will* be noticed.

2. **The Subject Line.** Since e-mail inboxes are so often cluttered, the subject line can provide a channel for you to express the intent of your letter and stand out in the crowd. This is particularly important in a business or volunteer sense, but it certainly can't hurt in day-to-day e-mailing. It's best to make your subject concise and meaningful, and please make sure it's correctly spelled and punctuated.

3. **The Reread Rule.** Don't hit "Send" until you've checked everything twice! Look for errors in spelling, grammar, and punctuation, as well as potential mistakes such as missing (or additional) attachments and incorrect addressees (oops!), and don't forget to check over the subject line. Remember, once you hit "Send," your missive is seconds away from arrival in the recipient's mailbox.

4. **Reply vs. Reply-All.** If you receive an e-mail that's been sent to several other people as well, you're at risk for sending what could be a personal response to a whole crowd of (possible) strangers. Hitting "Reply" will send your response *only* to the sender, whereas "Reply to All" includes *everyone* who received the first e-mail. Repeated misuse of "Reply to All" is a surefire way to annoy your unwitting recipients, appear unfamiliar with e-mail technology, and potentially reveal sensitive information about yourself without meaning to.

5. **Your Security.** E-mail, while popular and prevalent, is not the medium for confidential or legally sensitive information. If you're uncertain about the legality or sensitivity of what you're sending or forwarding, don't forward it on, or choose to convey important information a different way.

WHAT I LIKE ABOUT THE INTERNET: *New York Times* morning headlines and up-to-date news. Also, I can't take courses at the University without using the Internet. What I hate about the Internet: Passwords—there's no standardization of the requirements for number of letters, capitalization, etc.

—SAM KOSTICK
SEATTLE, WASHINGTON
YEARS RETIRED: *4*

• • • • • • • •

IF YOU CAN'T GET YOUR GRANDKIDS OFF THE COUCH, JOIN 'EM!

More than 19% of video game users are 50 and over, according to an Entertainment Software Association survey. As this sector has expanded, how is the industry responding? They're producing games to interest the 50+ set, and are even looking to senior gamers for opinions and reviews.

• • • • • • • •

I WAS AT A PARTY THE OTHER NIGHT. People were telling me that I knew so many different things. But that's because I sit and read online. Just because I read about this doesn't mean I can't read about that, by following a hyperlink. So technology expands my horizons of what I learn. If I were reading something in a book, I'd have to turn away from that book and look something up in an encyclopedia. Remember those days? Now it's a hyperlink. It's so much easier.

—BERYN HAMMIL
SAN FRANCISCO BAY AREA, CALIFORNIA

IT TOOK ME 30 SECONDS to make the transition to computers. I have been sitting in front of the keyboard since I was nine years old. I don't play a musical instrument; I play the typewriter. I love computers. It's really important for others to learn to send and receive e-mails. Someday even e-mails might become obsolete.

—MORT SHEINMAN
NEW YORK, NEW YORK
YEARS RETIRED: 10

. . . .

I MET AN ILLITERATE OLD MAN in a garbage dump in Indonesia. I helped him start a business and go back to his village. I e-mail with him. The e-mail goes to a local person who prints it out, rides 60 kilometers on his motorbike, and translates it into Bahasa for the old man. He gets the man's response in Bahasa, returns 60 kilometers on his bike, and sends me a translation by e-mail. We communicate even though the old man has never even touched a computer. I do this with a number of people whom I help. When the earthquake happened in Yushu, China, I raised about $4,000 from an e-mail I sent off to my donors. Within 24 hours, the money was in the hands of my contacts there, who could buy supplies to load in trucks and get them to the people in need. Without the Internet, this would never have happened.

—MARC GOLD
BANGKOK, THAILAND

. . . .

THE INTERNET HAS MADE A SIGNIFICANT DIFFERENCE. I'm now in touch with people all over the world, including those who used to work with me. For example, I am leaving for Europe on Friday and one of the places this cruise stops is Helsinki, Finland. I e-mailed a friend of mine whom I haven't seen in 25 years. Now he is meeting me at the boat when I get to Helsinki. And that's because of the Internet.

—BOB WALDORF
LOS ANGELES, CALIFORNIA
YEARS RETIRED: 11

More Wisdom: Lessons Learned

Wisdom is what we all strive for in life, and we certainly hope to grow smarter as we grow older. One difference (and I consider it a major improvement) is that in today's era of "pro-tirement," we can actually put all those life lessons we've learned right back into use. Now we know how to balance work and leisure, plan our finances wisely, get along with others, and savor the good times. As I said at the beginning of this book, we can own the future, and we should.

Listen to our respondents in this chapter. They're telling us over and over not to waste time and not to worry; to pursue our passions and never say we can't do something; to appreciate beauty and one another; and not to bother getting all those photos into albums, because we'll be way too busy to finish that job. And so, armed with the why and the how for this Third Phase of our lives, let's go live it.

IF YOU START DRESSING OLD, YOU *ARE* OLD. No matter how old she got, my mother never started dressing like my grandmother. She never dressed like an old person. I'll never stop wearing jeans and sneakers, no matter how old I get.

> —*L.H.*
> *BAZETTA, OHIO*
> *YEARS RETIRED: 1*

• • • • • • • •

HERE ARE MY "DON'TS." Don't let doctors' appointments become your social calendar. Don't take it personally when young people seem not to notice you; that's the way it goes, and besides, that's probably the way you were when you were their age. Don't shy away from new technology. You don't have to get into tweeting and texting and Facebooking and friending, but at least learn how to use e-mail; it's important.

Here are my "do's." Find something to do that gets you out of the house; find something that gives your day some structure. Keep moving. Remain as fit as you can, without overdoing it. Learn something new every day. Keep in touch with people, especially old friends, and don't be afraid to make new ones.

> —*MORT SHEINMAN*
> *NEW YORK, NEW YORK*
> *YEARS RETIRED: 10*

• • • • • • • •

LIFE IS ABOUT LIVING TODAY. The hell with tomorrow!

> —*SHIRLEY KELSO*
> *METHUEN, MASSACHUSETTS*
> *YEARS RETIRED: 20*

• • • • • • • •

THE BEST THING ABOUT BEING MY AGE: I've made most of the mistakes I will make in this lifetime.

> —*MAUREEN O'BOYLE*
> *NEW YORK, NEW YORK*
> *YEARS RETIRED: 6*

INDULGE YOURSELF. Enjoy listening to old-time jazz, read two papers a day, watch CNBC and C-SPAN, and even spend a whole afternoon with a juicy mystery. Do all the things you never could do before.

—*T.S.*
TAMPA, FLORIDA
YEARS RETIRED: 12

* * * * * * * *

WHILE YOU ARE ALIVE, WORRY ABOUT LIFE: You'll have plenty of time to worry about death when you are dead. I'm a big believer in the idea of self-fulfilling prophecies. I've been around too many people my age who spend too much time worrying about death. I believe that if you think about death, you will bring it on quicker. There's no need to worry about it because it's going to happen no matter what. No one has figured out a way to cheat death yet. I was at a meeting where this older gentleman told the group at least 10 times that he knew his days were numbered. That was all he could think about.

—*OTIS REQUISH*
POLAND, OHIO
YEARS RETIRED: 2

* * * * * * * *

SET GOALS FOR YOURSELF. Whether you set them monthly or yearly, it's important to keep yourself focused on something attainable, tangible. It's easy to get lulled into a life of inactivity with very little personal production. Each year I set goals for personal wealth, time spent on charity causes, and health factors like weight and cholesterol levels.

—*MARK HEDNASLER*
YOUNGSTOWN, OHIO
YEARS RETIRED: 4

* * * * * * * *

WHEN YOU LOSE A FRIEND, make another one.

—*MICHAEL CREEDMAN*
SAN FRANCISCO, CALIFORNIA

THE MOST IMPORTANT THING IS TO STAY AWAY from the "I can't do that because I'm too old" mind-set. Thinking like that can be hazardous to your health. I read twice a week to elementary school kids. Being around all of that energy and enthusiasm makes me feel young.

　　　—ANONYMOUS
　　　BALTIMORE, MARYLAND
　　　YEARS RETIRED: 13

DON'T BUY INTO THE AGEISM IN OUR CULTURE. Many people still see us as old and incapable of many things that we are more than capable of. If someone tells me I play tennis like a 55-year-old when I am 73, I don't consider that a compliment. I look them straight in the eye and say that an older person who has played tennis all her life can play tennis like this at 73. It is an ageist statement that assumes that one shouldn't be able to play tennis that well at 73. Baloney. People said I was too old to bike across America. I had osteoporosis. How would I get over the mountains? Well, I tell them that we might not be fast, but we have stamina and can outlast the best of them. Ageism is like racism, and it limits us.

　　　—EMILY KIMBALL
　　　RICHMOND, VIRGINIA

WHEN I RETIRED, SOME OF MY COLLEAGUES asked me what I was going to do first. I told them I didn't know, but I knew what I *wasn't* going to do: get a divorce, take up drinking, start smoking, or become a gambler, because they are all expensive, both to your health and pocketbook! I worked hard to have great golden years, and I'm not going to blow it now.

　　　—JIM EYRE
　　　JACKSONVILLE, TEXAS
　　　YEARS RETIRED: 6

I REALIZED WITHIN THE FIRST WEEK OF RETIREMENT
that taking care of myself in the morning—brushing
my teeth, washing up, getting dressed—was important, not just something to rush through because
I had to get to work. It was important to honor
myself enough to do those things. And when I
did, it made things more normal and pleasant.
Getting dressed, I am more apt to experience the
day spontaneously. I am ready for everything, to
go out if I need to, whether to go to the store
or to run errands, or just to take a walk. Sitting
around in sweatpants or pajamas is not condu-
cive to that.

> —*MICHAEL*
> *SAYVILLE, NEW YORK*
> *YEARS RETIRED: 1*

• • • • • • • • •

ATTITUDE IS THE KEY TO SUCCESSFUL RETIREMENT. You don't
have to do things that cost a lot of money. I love going on
picnics, taking walks, enjoying nature. That doesn't cost anything. People get so caught up in the traveling, in thinking
you have to go halfway around the world, when you can just
enjoy the place where you are.

> —*ANONYMOUS*
> *ST. PAUL, MINNESOTA*

• • • • • • • • •

HERE'S ONE THING I'VE LEARNED ABOUT RETIREMENT: You're
not going to get your photographs organized into albums.
People think that they're going to do that when they're
retired, but if they're not interested enough to have done it
before, they're not going to do it when they're retired, either.

> —*JANET*
> *MINNEAPOLIS, MINNESOTA*
> *YEARS RETIRED: 10*

THE COACH'S CORNER

MORE MEANINGFUL THAN MONEY

We are accustomed to the idea of leaving tangible assets to family members, organizations, and other worthy causes. This shows our commitment and is an important way in which to perpetuate our legacy.

But in addition to the assets described in a typical will, we all have so many memorable experiences and so much valuable advice to leave behind.

We have values—our real legacy—to communicate. We can share them through what is commonly referred to as an ethical will. Done properly, an ethical will creates a blueprint for a general will (which distributes the tangible goods) and for future generations.

A man I knew shared the important value of family time when he distributed the contents of his will. He asked that the whole family gather each year on the anniversary of his passing for a reunion and to share stories about him. This has now been going on for 45 years and has grown so large that the family now rents a large space for the gathering and everyone looks forward to it.

Ethical wills provide each one of us with the opportunity to communicate that which gives our life meaning—that which is painful, joyful—that which if only we knew when we were younger...well...

There is no one right way to write your ethical will, but here are some tips for getting started:

- If you have difficulty beginning, try writing it in the form of a letter to one of your heirs.
- Use favorite words or sayings that people associate with you or that are particularly meaningful to your family.
- Use anecdotes from your life.
- Include important dates from your life (for example, when you or a family member came to this country).
- Write in a style that reflects your personality— humor is great!

—B.W.

I **WORK IN RADIATION THERAPY,** and I can't tell you the number of people who have retired and then spent the next week with me getting radiation therapy treatments. I'm sure I wasn't the person they planned on retiring with. Don't put off all the fun trips, showing people love, living life while you are living day to day. Retirement can be very fun, and it's important to remember the saying, "Life is the journey." So many people don't get that concept until the end of their lives, and by then, you cannot go back and change anything you wished you would have done. Make every day count!

—K.J.H.
WESTERVILLE, OHIO

. . . .

I **WOULD SAY I AM BRAVER** now than I was before. I am willing to take chances: I have a deeper longing to live out what I really want to be a part of.

—MARCIA JAFFE
MILL VALLEY, CALIFORNIA

. . . .

RETIREMENT IS LIKE A FLOWER: It is constantly opening.

—J.L.
CENTRALIA, WASHINGTON
YEARS RETIRED: 9

DON'T THINK OF IT AS RETIRING FROM LIFE; it is just another phase of life. Take the energy you put into your work and put it into an activity you truly enjoy: taking courses, doing pottery, writing poetry, whatever. It is most important to give it your all and just consider it another aspect of your life.

—*BEVERLY ZEIDENBERG*
BETHESDA, MARYLAND
YEARS RETIRED: 2

RETIREMENT IS HEARING THE BIRDS SING, not having to lock my dogs up and leave them alone all day, sleeping in, long casual showers, yummy home cooking, not having to buy groceries with all the working crowd, no work evaluations, watering my plants as I drink my morning cup of coffee, time to pray and reflect, seeing my family more. Retirement is about making my own decisions at my own pace and having time to enjoy the world around me.

—*C.R.*
SAN ANTONIO, TEXAS
YEARS RETIRED: 1

MY GOALS WERE TO TAKE A DEEP BREATH, relax, and spend more time with my kids and for myself. It wasn't a long bucket list of all the things you want to do before you … I didn't look at it as that, because I am only 46 years old. I will have a new career and at some point I will likely retire again. It will be interesting to see how I do it the next time I retire.

—*MITCH COHEN*
MILL VALLEY, CALIFORNIA
YEARS RETIRED: 2

IN RETIREMENT, EVERY DAY IS SUNDAY. Who could complain about that?

—*ANONYMOUS*
NEW YORK, NEW YORK

RETIREMENT IS LIKE A VACATION FOR THE REST OF YOUR LIFE.
I'm happy that we had five good years together before my
husband got sick and passed away in 2002. Getting older
makes you more fully appreciate what you have, and you
have the time to enjoy it!

—BARBARA DICKERSON
OLD MINES, MISSOURI
YEARS RETIRED: 15

* * * * * * * *

IF YOU LET THE DAY UNFOLD, it has its own music. You just
have to sit and listen to it. There's so much beauty in not
planning the day. I think that's where I am now, and why I can
say I'm happy.

—MICHAEL
SAYVILLE, NEW YORK
YEARS RETIRED: 1

* * * * * * * *

KEEP REACHING OUT TO PEOPLE and respond to them when
they reach out to you. Be active. Don't sit in a corner and
read or watch TV. That's not the way to really enjoy life.

—FRANCES LOMAS FELDMAN
PASADENA, CALIFORNIA
YEARS RETIRED: 24

* * * * * * * *

STRIVE FOR A POSITIVE ATTITUDE. Sinking into feeling sorry for
oneself is a no-no.

—JOANN
JOPPA, MARYLAND
YEARS RETIRED: 9

* * * * * * * *

I AM IN TRANSITION. At 87, I know that sounds funny but I
surely feel that way. I must say my life has never been boring.

—SUE SIEGAL
SAN FRANCISCO, CALIFORNIA

EVER HEAR THE ONE ABOUT THE OLD COUPLE who were in bed together? The old wife raised the covers to look at her man and said, "You didn't save anything for retirement, did you?"

—*KENNETH R. WADE*
GATLINBURG, TENNESSEE
YEARS RETIRED: 1

* * * * * * * *

IN THE LONG RUN, doing a good job of raising your children is one of the best contributions you can make to the future of humankind. You never get to stop being a parent. You think one day they'll go off to college, get a job, and get on with their own lives. But they're never off your mind. You accumulate all this great advice that they don't want. But it's good to keep in touch, and it's good to love them and let them know that. For most of us, that's probably our major contribution to the world. Love your wife, take care of your children, take care of your community.

—*ROBERT L. ZIMDAHL*
FORT COLLINS, COLORADO
YEARS RETIRED: 1

* * * * * * * *

THE THING ABOUT RETIREMENT that has surprised me most is that after many, many years of being independent and having a lot of time to myself, I enjoy having my spouse around!

—*NOLA SMITH*
TAMPA, FLORIDA
YEARS RETIRED: 25

* * * * * * * *

IT IS UP TO EACH OF US to create our own destiny. We each need to plan ahead financially, physically, and emotionally, so we can continue purposeful and satisfying lives.

—*B.D.*
SEATTLE, WASHINGTON
YEARS RETIRED: 18

SO, WHY WORRY?

OVER THE LAST 30 YEARS OR SO, I have asked hundreds of people this question: "Can you name *just one time* in your entire life where worrying about an event changed its outcome?" No one has ever been able to name an event.

So, why worry? If you identify an event in your life that is bothersome, assess the event, and then ask yourself if you can do something about it. If you can change it, change it. If you can't change it, forget about it. If it then happens, deal with it. In general, people's lives would be so much happier if they didn't worry. Assess the event, do something about it or let it go. I have this discussion with a lot of people I meet in volunteer work. In most cases, they see the point and feel more in control of their lives.

I once asked a person if he was afraid of having a heart attack. He said he was. I asked what he was doing about it and he replied that he got stress tests every year, watched his blood pressure and cholesterol, had a glass of red wine every day, and got one hour of exercise every day. I asked what else he could do to prevent a heart attack and he said, "Nothing." He was doing everything he could to deal with heart attack risk, so why worry? *If* it ever happens, deal with it.

> —*BARRY BIANCO*
> *BRISTOL, WISCONSIN*
> *YEARS RETIRED: 2*

IF THE GOOD LORD MADE ANYTHING BETTER than sex and retirement, then He kept it for Himself! It just gets better and better!

—*CHALMERS GABLE*
MARION, TEXAS
YEARS RETIRED: 5

• • • • • • • •

LIFE IS VERY PRECIOUS. People don't take enough time to look at the sky and the stars and the moon and hug a tree once in a while. The other day I saw a kid kissing a tree. I thought, That's fantastic. What wonderful things the trees do for us; they clean the air and give us shade. We need to love each other and love our environment and our planet.

—*ROY CLARY*
BROOKLYN, NEW YORK
YEARS RETIRED: 1

• • • • • • • •

EVERY DAY, I WANT TO BE READY to experience whatever life throws my way.

—*MICHAEL*
SAYVILLE, NEW YORK
YEARS RETIRED: 1

• • • • • • • •

EVERY SINGLE DAY I LEARN SOMETHING NEW that is interesting, exciting, and of some importance. I am a believer in shaking up life and seeing what happens. Years ago, I said: OK, I'm not going to read fiction for the next six weeks. Or, I am not going to watch any TV at all for three weeks and see what I do to fill that time. Or, I am not going to eat meat: I became a vegetarian for eight years. All these various things put you in a position to open yourself up to new possibilities.

—*LIZ ALDERMAN*
ROCHESTER COUNTY, NEW YORK

WHAT MOTIVATES ME NOW? Just getting out of bed and remaining healthy and getting to spend quality time with my seven grandchildren. And now having the time and the opportunity to be a good role model in their lives. Getting to play a large role in their lives is great. I have found that now I can commit so much time to them without having to worry about getting to bed at a certain time because I have to work the next day. I can give myself completely to them, and that's a very unburdening feeling. I want to be able to watch them all grow up and get married and have children of their own. I'm motivated by the chance to be a great-grandmother.

—*J.E.*
MORGANTOWN, WEST VIRGINIA
YEARS RETIRED: 2

. . . .

DON'T POSTPONE. We don't live in a solid state. Life is changing. Live in the now.

—*EUGENE C. BIANCHI*
ATHENS, GEORGIA
YEARS RETIRED: 5

. . . .

YOU NEVER SEE BEAUTY until you've got the time to look.

—*BARBARA DICKERSON*
OLD MINES, MISSOURI
YEARS RETIRED: 15

. . . .

LIFE IS ABOUT ENDURING. And being temporary.

—*ROBERT DENIS*
SEATTLE, WASHINGTON
YEARS RETIRED: 24

. . . .

KEEP MOVING, KEEP DRINKING, and stop smoking. Have a good time!

—*ISABELLA HUTCHINGS*
METHUEN, MASSACHUSETTS
YEARS RETIRED: 30

THE BEST THING ABOUT RETIREMENT

I CAN DO WHAT I WANT. I play golf, smoke cigars, and travel with my wife. Also, now I get to read books. When I was working, I never had time for that.

> —*DAN PISANI*
> *MERIDEN, CONNECTICUT*
> *YEARS RETIRED: 1*

• • • • • • • • •

I'VE BECOME MUCH MORE INVOLVED WITH MY FAMILY. I spend more time with my grandkids, and at the end of the day, this is what's important.

> —*DOROTHY DURBIN GAUDIN*
> *TORONTO, ONTARIO*
> *YEARS RETIRED: 10*

• • • • • • • • •

THE BEST PART IS SLEEPING IN and showering, dressing, eating breakfast at my leisure. The worst part is that everyone thinks, "Oh, she is retired, I will just ask her to do this. She has so much time on her hands."

> —*C.R.*
> *SAN ANTONIO, TEXAS*
> *YEARS RETIRED: 1*

• • • • • • • • •

I DO THINGS WHEN I want to do them, not when I have to do them.

> —*M.K.*
> *SOUTHPORT, CONNECTICUT*
> *YEARS RETIRED: 12*

RECONNECTING WITH FRIENDS AND CLASSMATES from years ago is very rewarding.

—*ARTHUR KOFF*
CHICAGO, ILLINOIS

* * * * * * * *

I'M ABLE TO PURSUE MY TWO LOVES: music and gardening. I play the piano every day now and have season tickets to the symphony. I go to Duke Chapel every week, too, to hear the music there, which is amazing. I'm also able to spend more time in my yard gardening.

—*M.A.R.*
DURHAM, NORTH CAROLINA
YEARS RETIRED: 8

RETIREMENT IS FREEDOM. I do what I want to do. It's not that I hated working, but it was an obligation. I'm able to enjoy life more because I have the freedom to do what I want, and I'm young and healthy enough to enjoy it.

—*JAMES EVANS*
REPUBLIC, MISSOURI
YEARS RETIRED: 5

* * * * * * * *

WHAT DO I MISS SINCE I RETIRED? A paycheck, my boss, and the co-workers/friends whom I saw every day. But what a joy to just sit here in the morning, drink that cup of coffee, and see the younger people on their way to work.

—*RUTH BEARDEN*
JACKSONVILLE, TEXAS
YEARS RETIRED: 16

* * * * * * * *

IT IS YOUR *JOB* TO MAKE OLD AGE look really fun, so that everyone who looks up at it sees gray-haired, wrinkly people smiling and laughing!

—*CINDY JOSEPH*
NEW YORK, NEW YORK

WHILE WE WERE VACATIONING in Cabo San Lucas, Mexico, last month, we came across this quotation, which I think is something to consider when retiring: "Life should not be a journey to the grave with the intention of arriving safely in an attractive and well-preserved body, but rather you should skid in sideways, chocolate in one hand, martini in the other, body thoroughly used up, totally worn out, and screaming, 'Woo hoo! What a ride!' Life is not measured by the number of breaths we take, but by the moments that take our breath away."

—*KENNETH R. WADE*
GATLINBURG, TENNESSEE
YEARS RETIRED: 1

THE COACH'S TOOLBOX

WORKSHEETS, EXERCISES
AND INFORMATION FOR WRITING
THE NEXT CHAPTER OF YOUR LIFE

PLAN FOR YOUR RETIREMENT IN FIVE EASY STEPS

Still wondering if now is the time to finally call it quits (or rather, call it a new beginning)? We all need a little push. Here are some helpful tips to send you on your way.

1. Take the time to thoughtfully design this next stage of your life—identify passions and activities you may not have had time to pursue until now. Think about what factors will give your life a sense of meaning and purpose.

2. Meet with an accountant or financial adviser to determine whether you can successfully meet the financial requirements associated with this plan.

3. Determine whether you want a "bridge" career—something to ease you out of the workforce—or to stop completely. A bridge career may also provide incremental income you aren't ready to completely give up.

4. Create a wellness plan that includes an exercise and diet regimen to meet your individual needs. Consider wellness as encompassing your physical, emotional, spiritual, and intellectual self.

5. Develop and strengthen your emotional support networks—these relationships are critical to successful aging.

CHECKING UNDER THE HOOD: ARE YOU TAKING CARE OF YOURSELF?

So many of us put off taking care of ourselves while we are working full-time. No more excuses: Be honest with yourself in answering these questions and think about what you might do to better support yourself.

1. What is the current state of your general health?

2. Do you get enough sleep?

3. Do you wake up feeling refreshed?

4. Do your eating habits reflect your dietary requirements and keep you at a healthy weight?

5. Have you had a health checkup in the past year?

6. Do you have a regular exercise routine that increases your heart rate for approximately 30 minutes? If so, how many times per week do you exercise?

7. Are you attending to your spiritual or purposeful self?

8. Are you engaging in stimulating activities that cause you to learn new things and stretch yourself intellectually?

9. How is your stress level? What are some healthy ways you have found to deal with stress in your life?

LIFE BALANCE EXERCISE

The sections of the wheel below represent balance and fulfillment. This exercise helps you better understand how
you are spending your time. It also helps you be more
thoughtful about how you actually feel about various aspects
of your life. It helps to identify what's working, what's not,
and where you might want to begin to make some changes.

Regarding the center of the wheel as 0 and the outer edges
as 10, rank your degree of satisfaction with each area by
drawing a line to create a new outer edge. Use a different
color for each piece of the pie. If these titles don't reflect
your life, fill in your own. The new perimeter of the circle will
illustrate the balance you have in your life. How bumpy would
the ride be if this were a real wheel?

WHEEL OF BALANCE

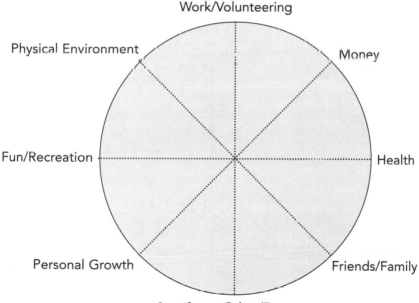

KNOW WHEN TO HOLD 'EM AND WHEN TO FOLD 'EM

Making lists is a powerful way to clarify your thoughts. Create this chart to help you visualize how you may make changes in the future. Indicate how you can begin to restructure and improve your life by listing activities that fit in each of the four categories below and on the next page.

HOLD ON	LET GO

PLANNING WORKSHEET

As you begin to plan for retirment, a funny thing happens: You tend to want to simplify. As you envision your future and develop new goals, explore how you might simplify your life, on a global as well as an everyday basis.

ADD	QUESTION

TO MOVE OR NOT TO MOVE: THAT IS THE QUESTION

After completing the Wheel of Balance exercise, take a look at how you rated your physical environment. Then investigate further by asking yourself these questions:

1. What do you like about your immediate neighborhood? Your town?

2. How do you feel about the current level of upkeep necessary for your home?

3. In thinking about your finances, does the overhead associated with maintaining your home significantly minimize other choices you make about things you would like to do?

4. What do you like about your current home? What would you change?

5. Think about other things you have wanted to do in your home—clean out the clutter, for instance?

6. Allow yourself to dream: Is there someplace or some type of living environment you've always wanted to experience but had too many responsibilities, forcing you to say no?

A COACH'S GUIDE TO MAKING YOUR WISDOM WORK FOR YOU

There's more to preparing for this next stage of life than financial planning and physical fitness. While you're getting organized, don't forget to accomplish some spring-cleaning on your inner self. Here are some tools for the job:

1. Listen to messages you've gotten from your most significant mentors. These might include your third-grade teacher, a friend, a religious leader, and the like. Who are they and what core message resonated with you? How can you integrate that learning into your life?

2. The arts are a powerful tool for reflection and can open avenues for personal exploration and growth. Core meaning is expressed by all cultures through the use of music, poetry, art, and stories. Reconnect with some aspect of the arts and see what it teaches you. Have you always dreamed of singing? Painting? Writing?

3. Accept yourself inside and out. It takes courage to make peace with yourself, and the third stage of life is a gift of time and opportunity to develop increased clarity about what you choose to do and create with what you've got.

4. Identify your core passions and sense of purpose. Think about what gifts and talents you possess—even those you've never used before. Use these as a launching pad as you design the post-career life you'd like to lead.

5. Shift from a J-O-B to your real life's work. As Tara Mohr points out, "Real work is what you are called to do, the work that feels right in your soul."

ANNUAL GOAL-SETTING WORKSHEET

Think about where you would like to be in your life in one year. What goals do you want to achieve? Be realistic and don't bite off more than you can chew. Make your goals SMART: Specific, Measurable, Achievable, Realistic, and Time-oriented.

Date: _____

Work: _____
_____
_____
_____
_____
_____
_____

Family/Relationships: _____
_____
_____
_____
_____
_____
_____

Health/Fitness: _____
_____
_____
_____
_____
_____
_____

Spirituality: _____

_____

_____

_____

_____

_____

_____

Civic Engagement: _____

_____

_____

_____

_____

_____

_____

Fun/Travel/Recreation: _____

_____

_____

_____

Lifelong Learning: _____

_____

_____

_____

_____

Other: _____

_____

_____

_____

_____

_____

KEYS TO MAKING RETIREMENT THE BEST YEARS OF YOUR LIFE

1. *Understand yourself and what drives you.* Is your identity governed by your title at work? The stories we hear about people dropping dead the day after retirement are most often just urban legends, but some people do feel tremendous stress when they are cut off from an extremely important part of their lives. Let's face it; many of us spend more hours at work than anywhere else. Pre-plan a shift toward identifying yourself in a different way. Working with a life-transition coach can be particularly helpful at this juncture; a coach can help crystallize just who you want to be, now that you are a grown-up!

2. *Before you leave your job, find activities that will be fulfilling.* One of the most satisfying and useful ways to support a change in identity from work to retirement is to try new things. Become a renaissance man or woman as you dabble in the arts, in travel, in all sorts of new activities. Or redirect your professional energies into a bridge career or volunteer job. Rather than identifying just one focus, allow yourself to explore and discover what you might like to do with your time; and, just as important, what you will shy away from.

3. *Understand and prepare for the natural change in family dynamics.* The anecdotes about retirement as today's number-one threat to health may not be true, but the old adage, "I married you for better or worse, but not for lunch," is something I hear from clients all the time! An unanticipated source of stress for retirees and their loved ones can be the tendency to want to spend all of their time together. Communication is vital—talk about expectations you each have about time spent together and shifting household responsibilities. Also consider the needs of extended family members: parents and children. They may be looking forward to spending more time with you or getting more help from you. How will this fit into your overall

plan?

4. *Develop new social outlets.* Many of us develop friendships around the water cooler and miss that interaction
once we retire. Having more time enables you to deepen
existing relationships, attend to broken ones, and develop
new friendships based on common interests and activities.
Women tend to be more adept at this than men, but
expanding social outlets is just as important for men once
relationships are no longer centered around the office.

5. *Create a solid financial plan.* It's been estimated that
retirees should expect to generate 80–100% of their pre-
retirement income in order to maintain a comfortable
lifestyle. This requires the 3 Ps: Planning, Perseverance,
and Plenty of sources of income. Along with Social
Security, pension, IRA and 401K monies, look to make
investments that will make a steady return.

NUMBERS DON'T LIE

Most people nearing retirement age don't really know their net worth. This number is a crucial first step in determining if you are financially ready to retire. Here's a simple way to get started: Subtract your total debts from total assets to determine your net worth.

ASSETS	NAME/VALUE
Real Estate Holdings	
Automobiles	
Jewelry, Antiques, Art	
Money Market Funds	
Other Funds (CDs)	
Life Insurance	
IRA Accounts	
Pension/Profit Sharing Plans	
401K Plan	
Investments:	
Stocks	
Bonds	
Property	
Business Equity	
Trusts	
Other	
TOTAL ASSETS	

DEBTS	NAME/VALUE
Mortgage	
Loans:	
Car	
Education	
Home Equity	
Other	
Alimony/Child Support	
Credit Card Debt	
Other	
TOTAL DEBTS	
NET WORTH	

FINANCIAL CHECKUP FOR PRE-RETIREES

A retiree's financial plan should yield an income stream of between 80–100% of pre-retirement income in order to live comfortably. The following questions will help you determine how close you are to that goal:

1. Determine your post-retirement lifestyle and associated expenses. Will you be traveling more or less? Eating out more or less? You will probably be spending more money on recreation. How do these changes compare to your current cost of living?

2. Determine your specific retirement benefits. These include Social Security, pensions, IRAs, 401K plans, investments, annuities, and more. There have been a number of changes over the past few years, particularly as they relate to health care. Know what you are entitled to and what you can depend upon.

3. Create a plan for health care and long-term care coverage and determine costs associated with these areas. Don't forget about the high cost of prescription drugs.

4. Consider how any emergency expenses will be handled and prepare a contingency plan to handle this.

5. Look at your own family. Are you likely to be more or less financially responsible for other family members during your retirement years?

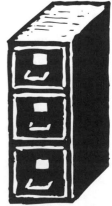

FINDING THE RETIREMENT PLACE OF YOUR DREAMS

B*aby boomers—the generation on the cusp of retirement— are proactively seeking their individually perfect retirement location, and their standards are high. How do you go about figuring out if you're making the right decision? Here are some suggestions.*

1. *Expenses:* Check out the work options, housing prices, and tax rates for any place you're considering.

2. *Community:* Research the demographics of your location (go to the Census Bureau's website) to find out about your new neighbors. Visit the local Chamber of Commerce website as well, and pick up a copy of the local and regional newspapers to learn about issues, events, and other items of importance to residents.

3. *Health and Wellness:* Find out how far away the best hospital or medical center is, and check that institution to make sure it has the most up-to-date facilities and staff. websites devoted to alternative health can help you make sure you'll have easy access to practitioners.

4. *Learning and Education:* Investigate the local opportunities for continuing education, especially degree-granting institutions. Access to a major university will bring a broad range of benefits to older local residents beyond classes and courses.

5. *Transportation:* Make sure you have access to reliable local public transportation: You won't want to have to drive everywhere. Weigh the advantages and disadvantages of relocating far from a major airport hub or rail line.

6. *Environment:* Some people can't live without the change of seasons; others have had enough of snow and ice, or heat and rain. Make sure you know what you're getting into, weather-wise. While you're at it, check out any new location for the kind of details that are rarely mentioned by real estate agents: Superfund cleanup sites, nuclear power plants, plutonium storage facilities, or wilderness acreage that's not legally protected.

7. *Quality-of-Life Details:* What enhances your life? Don't assume your new place will offer those little things that mean a lot to you: great cappuccino, a cozy used-book store, inspiring yarn shop, spicy Indian food, enticing hiking trail, or restful public garden. Make your list of small-but-essential features, and check them off as you find them.

FIND WHAT YOU NEED ONLINE

There's a wealth of information on the Web about any activity you may want to investigate. Try these sites to start; they'll lead you to more.

VOLUNTEERING

International Executive Service Corps
www.iesc.org

Global Volunteers
www.globalvolunteers.org

Habitat for Humanity
www.habitat.org

Civic Ventures
www.civicventures.org

HandsOn Network
www.handsonnetwork.org

Experience Corps
www.experiencecorps.org

Americorps
www.americorps.gov

Age4Action Network
www.age4action.org/resources-serve.html

TRAVEL

Seniors Home Exchange
www.seniorshomeexchange.com

Grand Travel
www.grandtrvl.com

FINANCIAL

Investopedia
www.investopedia.com/articles/retirement

CNN Money
www.money.cnn.com/retirement/

findingDulcinea Finance Guide: Retirement Planning
www.findingdulcinea.com/guides/Finance/Retirement-
Planning.pg_00.html

New York Times/Your Money Guide: Retirement
www.topics.nytimes.com/your-money/retirement/index.html

EDUCATION

Road Scholar (formerly Elderhostel)
www.roadscholar.org

Senior Net
www.seniornet.org

Osher Foundation/Osher Lifelong Learning Institutes
www.osherfoundation.org/index.php?olli_list
usm.maine.edu/olli/national

FOR WOMEN

WomanSage
www.womansage.com

Red Hat Society
www.redhatsociety.org

National Women's Health Network
www.nwhn.org

The Transition Network
www.thetransitionnetwork.org

GENERAL INTEREST

American Society on Aging
www.asaging.org

National Council on Aging
www.ncoa.org

American Association of Retired Persons (AARP)
www.aarp.org

GREAT SITES FROM OUR INTERVEWEES

You've read their stories and advice in these pages; to find out more about their work, their inspiration and their achievements, visit their websites.

Liz and Steven Alderman
www.petercaldermanfoundation.org/

Marc Gold
www.100friends.org/

Dore Hammond
www.dorehammondfilms.com/

Marcia Jaffe
www.baliinstitute.org/

Cindy Joseph
www.boombycindyjoseph.com

Tim Will
www.farmersfreshmarket.org/rutherford/

SPECIAL THANKS

Thanks to our intrepid "headhunters" for going out to find so many respondents from around the country with interesting advice to share:

Jamie Allen, Chief Headhunter

Andrea Blum
Andrea Fine
Andrea Syrtash
Beshaleba Rodell
Connie Farrow
Helen Bond
Jen Hinger
Jennifer Bright
 Reich

Jenny McNeill-
 Brown
Jody Shenn
Kazz Regelman
Ken McCarthy
Laura Stevens
Linda Lincoln
Lisa Jaffe Hubbell

Natasha
 Lambropoulos
Nicole Colangelo-
 Lessin
Patricia Woods
Shannon Hurd

Thanks, too, to our editorial advisor Anne Kostick. And thanks to our assistant, Miri Greidi, for her yeoman's work at keeping us all organized. The real credit for this book, of course, goes to all the people whose experiences and collective wisdom make up this guide. There are too many of you to thank individually, but you know who you are.

CREDITS

Page 5   www.RetirementPlanner.org.
Page 6   "The State of Retirement Planning," by Emily
              Brandon, US News and World Report online
Page 13   "Prime Time: Follow these steps to a happy
              retirement" by Emily Brandon, US News and
              World Report online
Page 15   "The New Retirement Mindscape. A ground-
              breaking, comprehensive study of the retire-
              ment journey" by Ameriprise Financial in con-
              junction with Age Wave and Ken Dychtwald,
              Ph.D. and Harris Interactive, Inc.,
Page 16   "The New Retirement Mindscape"
Page 25   "Prime Time: Follow these steps to a happy
              retirement"
Page 26   "Today's Retirement Journey: Forget those
              stereotypes." by Betsy Streisand, US News and
              World Report online
Page 31   "The New Retirement Mindscape"
Page 33   "The New Retirement Mindscape"
Page 39   "The New Retirement Mindscape"
Page 56   "Volunteering: Priceless Experience for Free,"
              by Jeff Yeager, www.aarp.org
Page 64   "Presto Change-O," by Samuel Greengard,
              www.aarpmagazine.org/money/recareering.html
Page 97   "Healthy Retirement Tips", US News and
              World Report online
Page 98   "Older Americans and Mature Pets," The
              Humane Society of the United States,
              www.hsus.org
Page 105   "Fat 2 Fit: Get Smarter and Perform Better—
              Exercise!" by Carole Cason, AARP.org.
Page 120   "Make New Friends, Get Involved" by Michelle
              Diament, AARP Bulletin Today
Page 125   www.AARP.org
Page 127   "Today's Retirement Journey: Forget those
              stereotypes."
Page 137   www.AARP.org.
Page 147   www.AARP.org.

BE THE CHANGE!

Change the World. Change Yourself.

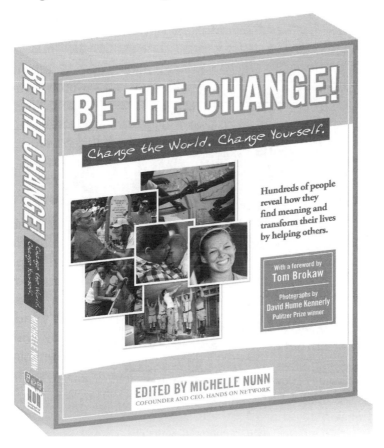

By intertwining practical advice on service and volunteerism with real-life stories of personal transformation, this book is the perfect companion for people who want to be inspired and informed and to take action to change their lives and their world. **Edited by Michelle Nunn, Co-founder and CEO of Hands On Network.**

"This is a wonderful and inspiring book."

—*WALTER ISAACSON CEO, ASPEN INSTITUTE*

"This is a book that could change your life … It's almost magic and it could happen to everyone. Go!"

—*JIM LEHRER, ANCHOR, PBS NEWSHOUR WITH JIM LEHRER*

WHAT THE CRITICS ARE SAYING ABOUT HUNDREDS OF HEADS®

"The next 'Dummies' or 'Chicken Soup' … offers funny but blunt advice from thousands across America who've walked some of life's rougher roads."
　　—*DEMOCRAT AND CHRONICLE (ROCHESTER, NEWYORK)*

"Colorful bits of advice…So simple, so entertaining, so should have been my million-dollar idea."
　　—*THE COURIER-JOURNAL (LOUISVILLE, KENTUCKY)*

"The books have struck a nerve. 'Freshman Year' was the number-one-selling college life guide … "
　　——*CNN.COM*

"The series … could be described as 'Chicken Soup for the Soul' meets 'Worst Case Scenario.'"
　　—*ATLANTA BUSINESS CHRONICLE*

"Move over, 'Dummies' … Can that 'Chicken Soup!' Hundreds of Heads are on the march to your local bookstore!"
　　—*ELIZABETH HOPKINS, KFNX (PHOENIX, ARIZONA) RADIO HOST, THINKING OUTSIDE THE BOX*

"Hundreds of Heads hopes to make life in our complicated new millennium a bit more manageable."
　　—*THE RECORD (HACKENSACK, NEW JERSEY)*

About the Contributors

Peggy Brick, M.Ed., CSE, is an educational consultant specializing in sexuality across the lifespan. The founder and president of the Consortium on Sexuality and Aging, www.sexualityandaging.com, she teaches a popular course, "Older, Wiser, Sexually Smarter," at the Academy of Lifelong Learning, University of Delaware. She has received numerous awards for her leadership in the field of human sexuality during the past forty years, has trained thousands of educators and health care professionals across the nation, and is co-author of numerous popular teaching manuals including "Older, Wiser, Sexually Smarter: 30 Sex Ed Lessons for Adults Only."

Rosemary Cox, LCSW, Master's in Counseling and Human Services, Bachelor's in Secondary Education, certified Sageing Leader, and adjunct faculty member at Holy Cross College (Notre Dame, Indiana), is an educator and program designer for Memorial BrainWorks in South Bend, Indiana. She has worked in the aging field for 18 years and in the area of brain health and development for seven years. In addition to presenting at national and regional conferences, Rosemary has facilitated workshops and train-the-trainer seminars across the country. She has written facilitator manuals on the topics of memory improvement, stress management, and the cultivation of wisdom in the second half of life. Rosemary Cox has developed and coordinated several intergenerational programs. www.memorialbrainworks.com

Kathy Dragon, founder and owner of TravelDragon.com (http://TravelDragon.com), and The Dragon's Path (www.thedragonspath.com), has been creating and leading small group adventures around the world for the past two decades, personally escorting more than 3,000 "retired and retirement-age" travelers. She is a frequent international speaker and consultant specializing in the influence of boomers on travel and social media.

Gian Gonzaga, Ph.D., is a social-personality psychologist and head of research at eHarmony Labs. He has been studying emotion, relationships, health, and marriage for more than 20 years. www.eharmony.com

Henry S. Lodge, M.D., is the co-author of the *New York Times* bestseller *Younger Next Year,* and *Younger Next Year for Women.* He is an Associate Clinical Professor of Medicine at Columbia University, and a Board-certified internist in practice in New York City, where he heads a multi-specialty group practice. He is recognized in *Who's Who in Science and Engineering, in America, and in the World,* and in the

Best Doctors in America, and is a contributing editor for *SELF maga-zine*. You can read more of his work at www.youngernextyear.com.

Julie Lopp was raised in Minnesota, taught language arts in California, worked in public relations and advertising, and enjoyed a minor career in theater, radio, and TV. She is currently the owner of JoMax Property Management Co. and founder of Grandma's Enterprises, specializing in candy manufacturing in high-volume tourist retail stores. Her career transition was as the Executive Director of Life Plan Center in San Francisco, a national nonprofit offering career and life-planning services for men and women age 50 and older. She currently lives in Santa Barbara, California, where she consults and provides workshops dealing with internships for men and women in mid- and later life. www.InternShop.us

Debra Raybold is Director of Memorial BrainWorks, a program within Memorial Hospital of South Bend dedicated to extending cognitive health and reducing incidents of Alzheimer's and other dementias. BrainWorks offers educational programs, training, and national pro-grams and resources for those who wish to learn about applying the insights from neuroscience into day-to-day applications for a healthy brain lifestyle and healthy aging. More information and resources on brain healthy aging may be found at www.memorialbrainworks.com. She is also an individual and organizational coach, and the founder of That Essential Spark (www.thatessentialspark.com), working with indi-viduals to design and live fulfilling and meaningful lives.

Craig Trojahn is a National Life and Financial Services Trainer with Farmers Insurance Group. With his specialty being in the areas of busi-ness, estate and personal planning, Craig works directly with the Farmers Agency Force to coach them in the key features of the numer-ous products available, the effective use of each product, and how to present these products to their clients. Prior to Farmers, Craig was a Financial Planner with Prudential Financial. As a planner, his passion for providing top-notch service won him a loyal and varied clientele.

Susan Ayers Walker, BSEE, MSCS, is a journalist, consultant, and speaker. She has written for BoomerGadget, AARP.com and *AARP The Magazine*, Caring.com, and American Society on Aging Newsletter on technology for older adults. She is a nationally known speaker on aging-in-place technologies and has appeared on television and radio talk shows. She is the cofounder and managing director of the SmartSilvers Alliance (www.smartsilvers.com), whose mission is to promote technolo-gies that foster independence and quality of life for older adults. She is also the co-producer of the SilversSummit (www.silverssummit.com) at the Consumer Electronic Conference each year.

About the Special Editor

Barbara Waxman, MS, MPA, ACC, is the founder and president of the Odyssey Group, an executive and life coaching company for adults "midlife and better." Barbara works with businesses around the globe, supporting executives to increase their leadership ability and to enhance their self-awareness in order to maximize their capacity to succeed at home and at work.

As a personal coach, Barbara leads workshops, is a popular keynote speaker and works one-on-one with individuals wanting to design a life in sync with their sense of values, energy, purpose and potential. As an expert in adult development, Barbara infuses her coaching work with all she has learned about aging, wisdom and harnessing the potential of all we've learned as adults.

Barbara is a certified Executive and Personal Coach from both the Hudson Institute of Santa Barbara and the International Coach Federation. She holds a faculty position with GILD (Global Institute for Leadership Development) and is a Wexner Heritage fellow.

Barbara has frequently been called upon as an expert source and has contributed to eHarmony.com, First30Days.com, advice.com and other websites. She has appeared on Leeza Gibbons's *Hollywood Confidential* radio program, and has written numerous articles.

Originally from New York, Barbara lives with her family in Northern California.